Contents

Editorial

Kay Ryan	4	Two Poems
Dennis O'Driscoll	6	Poem: *Taskmasters*
Seán Haldane	8	*This Thing: Robert Graves and the Goddess*
Robert Selby	25	Poem: *Splendour*
Anne Stevenson	26	Two Poems
Rory Waterman	27	Poem: *Reverdie*
Dana Gioia	28	Poem: *The Argument*
Antonio Machado	29	Poem: *Traveler*, translated by Dana Gioia
Marcia Menter	30	*The Accessibility of Anthony Hecht*
Kevin Hanson	43	Poem: *Nietzsche and the Horse*
Travis Mossotti	44	Poem: *Delivering the Bad News*
Philip Rush	45	Poem: *Mimo*
Katrina Naomi	46	Poem: *The Woman who Married the Berlin Wall*
Kona Macphee	47	Two Poems
Richard Wilbur	48	On Creating Candide: An Interview
Angela Leighton	55	Poem: *Fen Elegy*
A. B. Jackson	56	Two Poems
Helena Nelson	58	*Blackadder, Polypton and Fruitcake*
Richie McCaffery	69	Poem: *The Rapture*
Claire Askew	70	Poem: *Dream Lover*
Niall Campbell	71	Poem: *The Fraud*
Alasdair Macrae	72	*The Law and Some Grace: Iain Crichton Smith*
Jack B. Bedell	79	Poem: *Economics*
Tony Roberts	80	*Matthew Arnold: A Taste in my Mind*
Julie Kane	90	*Mortality and Mellowing: On Wendy Cope*
Dick Davis	95	Poem: *Wil Mills*
	96	Notes on Contributors

D1437984

Editor · GERRY CAMBRIDGE
Editorial Assistant · TANYA WHITE
U.S. Assistant Editor · JENNIFER GOODRICH
U.S. Contributing Editor · MARCIA MENTER

EDITORIAL ADDRESSES

UK

Gerry Cambridge
3-A Blantyre Mill Road
Bothwell
South Lanarkshire
G71 8DD
Scotland.
e: gerry.cambridge@btinternet.com

USA

Jennifer Goodrich
70 Lincoln Avenue
Hastings-on-Hudson
New York 10706.
e: jlgtdh@aol.com

Marcia Menter
e: mlmtdh@verizon.net

WEBSITES

www.thedarkhorsemagazine.com
Facebook: The Dark Horse Magazine

SUBSCRIPTION DETAILS

The Dark Horse is a biannual publication. A subscription covers three issues to reduce administration. A British subscription costs £18. An American subscription is $28. Subscribe securely online here:

www.thedarkhorsemagazine.com/subscribe

or, alternatively, make cheques payable to 'Dark Horse Writers'. Institutional and single copy rates are available on our website.

GUIDELINES FOR CONTRIBUTORS

Our preference is to respond by email to all work submitted, and to recycle unused typescripts. If contributors would like unused submissions to be returned they should include sufficient return postage or International Reply Coupons and a self-addressed envelope.

Please allow ten weeks for consideration of your work. If you have still to hear from us, a reminder by email after this period is appropriate and welcomed.

Unsolicited submissions by email are not accepted. Hard copy only, please, in the first instance.

© The Dark Horse & Contributors

Summer / Autumn 2011

Opinions expressed by contributors are not necessarily those of the editors.

In addition to the support of subscribers, a contribution from Creative Scotland aids the publication of this issue.

ALBA | CHRUTHACHAIL

TYPESET AND DESIGNED by GERRY CAMBRIDGE

PRINTED AND BOUND BY CHARLESWORTH PRESS

The Dark Horse Editorial

THE BREVITY OF LITERARY STANDING: as Alasdair Macrae points out in his essay-review on the late, and to my mind, great Iain Crichton Smith, a poetic reputation can these days fade rapidly when the poet no longer exists as a living presence. There are exceptions, of course: I've just returned from Orkney, my first visit to the islands since the day of George Mackay Brown's funeral in April 1996; there, George still feels very much a living part of the place—or a living absence—though his wider fame is possibly more for his fiction and other writings than for his poetry. The interest stirred up by Ron Ferguson's recent biographical accounting, *The Wound and the Gift*, demonstrates the reading public's depth of engagement with the Orkney writer. Would there be similar interest in a biography of Iain? He is, surely, equally a major writer—and in fiction, too: read his breathtaking short story 'Murdo' if you doubt it—and one whose work issued from a far less settled world view owing to his own island childhood and the choices he made as a result. This, you could say, makes him much more typical of a 'modern' Western sensibility: provisional, uncertain, agnostic and self-reliant. And what of Hugh MacDiarmid? He once remarked that, in Burns, Scotland had a great popular poet; it was his, MacDiarmid's, ambition to be Scotland's great *unpopular* poet. It seems he has thoroughly fulfilled this ambition. One gets little sense of him at present in the air in Scotland, nor, either, of those other related figures, Robert Garioch and Sydney Goodsir Smith.

It's to be seen how Edwin Morgan's poetry—the poet died just over a year ago—will fare. The poet was in the news recently, but not for his work. He left over £2,000,000 in his will, which caused journalistic mutterings that this socially-minded poet had been, lifelong, a secret venture capitalist. But no; the bulk of it was a portfolio of investments left to him by his parents. Under the terms of Morgan's will around half of it was donated to the Scottish National Party. Most of the remainder is, remarkably, for the establishment of an annual prize to publish the work of a Scottish poet under the age of thirty, though I gather 'Scottish' will be interpreted generously: if you live here, or if your granny, say, was Scottish, you can be considered so. The dearth of gifted young poets here, at least in terms of winning England-based literary prizes, has been something of a truism for the past fifteen years. Three interesting Scottish poets still in their twenties appear in this issue: Claire Askew, Richie McCaffery and Niall Campbell. It will be fascinating to see if the spin-off from EM's bequest kick-starts a new, age-related poetry renaissance north of the border; if money can be the handservant of the art and not, as one can sometimes think in more cynical moments, its master.

Kay Ryan

Putting Things in Proportion

The tree must be
bigger than
the house, the
doors of which
must fix upon
a width proportionate
to people. Objects
in the rooms
must coexist.
A kettle can't
be bigger than
a table. Interiors
must fit inside
in general. With
spaces left besides.
Swift justice to
rogue sizes, is what
we say—we have to
say. No one can
get along the
other way.

Ship in a Bottle

It seems
impossible—
not just a
ship in a
bottle but
wind and sea.
The ship starts
to struggle—an
emergency of the
too realized we
realize. We can
get it out but
not without
spilling its world.
A hammer tap
and they're free.
Which death
will it be,
little sailors?

Kay Ryan will be reading from her work
at 7.30pm on Wednesday, 9th of November 2011 at
The Scottish Storytelling Centre,
43–45 High Street, Edinburgh, EH1 1SR.
Tickets £7 / £5.

Dennis O'Driscoll

Taskmasters

Now that your nose is to the cornerstone,
you'll stay the course, top off each block
with slops of mortar, bring down the trowel's
iron discipline like a ton of bricks.
And soon you're in the swing of things,
absorbed by what you'd dreaded,
content as someone settling in a train,
aromatic latte in hand, newspaper
and glossy mag secured underarm,
moist caesar salad sandwich in reserve
behind protective cellophane—
an emergency lever encased in glass.

❖

Spring's surge of hormonal urgency
has long abated as you succumb
to ennui, wondering what you'd
ever seen in that hyperactive season.
Winter's scorched-earth policy takes hold
with a vengeance now, killing off everything
unable to fight back through hardy networks
of roots, brutal bare-knuckle thorns.
Snow flaking from damp walls of cloud,
the ascendant moon assuming pole position,
you abandon every pretence at outdoor
chores, build up defences from
the stockade of logs—the past year's
hatchet jobs—you'd laid in for
the open fireplace of your tied cottage.
You might decide to sketch out plans
for next summer's borders, browse
online catalogues of exotic shrubs.
But chances are you'll just lounge there

on the leather couch, tap into a glass
of home brew or boil the kettle for a warm-up
snorter of hot whiskey, deplete your stocks
of heather honey, lemons, cloves.

❧

Oh for the gift of eptitude. No task too big or small or awkward.
As nifty with a reciprocating saw as with a humble bradawl.
Adept at fitting unfamiliar widgets instinctively in place.
No ceiling, joist, masonry or quarry tile an impediment.
Marking out a rebated joint one day, knuckling down
to a cavity tray the next; checking the leak from a valve
spindle, then flush-mounting a socket outlet nearby.
Keeping the show on the road, the jets in the air,
the world's motor lubricated, its axis oiled; waving
aside the clients' plaudits, though their bafflement
is absolute when that guiding hand withdraws.
But by then their lives are set to rights: piped water
sourced again, heat coursing through radiators, the car's
smutty engine blasting off with rejuvenated smoothness.

❧

Then wrapping up a job, settling the tools in
the metal box, folding paint-drooled drop-cloths,
snapping the padlock back on the garden shed,
hosing down your splattered boots, changing
into a fabric-softened cotton polo shirt.
Even clicking the cap on the felt-tip, after
you sign off on the planning application.
Filing invoices, certificates, receipts
once the online tax form is completed
and the *Send* button flicked with relief.
Unwonted moments when all the pieces
cohere, loose ends tie up, quandaries resolve.

Seán Haldane

This Thing: Robert Graves and the Goddess

> All saints revile her, and all sober men
> Ruled by the God Apollo's golden mean—
> In scorn of which I sailed to find her
> In distant regions likeliest to hold her
> Whom I desired above all things to know,
> Sister of the mirage and echo...

ROBERT GRAVES STATED THAT 'the test of a poet's vision ... is the accuracy of his portrayal of the White Goddess and the island over which she rules', and that 'he must address only the Muse... and tell her the truth about himself and her.' His poem 'The White Goddess', written in middle age—in the first person, as above: the 'I' was later revised to 'we'—is by his own standards definitive. But 'He can't mean it' was the most heard comment on his lectures when he was Professor of Poetry at Oxford in the early 1960s—mainly from students reading English and well stuck in what he anachronistically described as 'Apollo's golden mean'. But his lectures were always packed, and in the main by students from other disciplines than literature: scientists often took him seriously—as did the faculty of MIT in 1963 when after due acknowledgment that 'true originality implies a leap taken by the mind across a dark gulf of nothingness into new regions of scientific thought', he explained that 'Symptoms of the trance in which poetic composition occurs differ greatly from those in an induced mediumistic trance; though both seem directed by an external power. In a poetic trance, which happens no more predictably than an epileptic fit, this power is traditionally identified with the ancient Muse-goddess.' For he did mean it, though his language of description could vary between the mythological and the straightforwardly puzzled and down to earth. When I first met him in 1961, I mentioned I had recently heard a reading on the BBC of one of his poems, 'Lion Lover', in which he describes 'gnawing bones in a dry lair' as well as 'your naked feet upon my scarred shoulders.' 'Read it very sexily, did he?' Graves asked. Then more seriously, 'It's bloody horrible. The awful thing is that you're in love with someone, even if you know she is completely heartless... There's this thing—call it the Goddess—always behaving absolutely bloodily. But you've got to . . .' He stopped. 'It gets worse and worse as you get older.'

Graves's reputation is now in flux. Since he died at the age of 90 in 1985, with dementia, this dementia is conjectured to have extended back to the years of his mad behaviour with young women he regarded as incarnations of the Muse. His frankness (he described *The White Goddess* as 'a crazy book') didn't help, nor did his obvious enjoyment of fame (being on the cover of *Life* magazine with a photo of him clambering in bathing trunks along a cliff face in Mallorca) during a period when media celebrity was being invented, nor did his being surrounded by various parasites and opportunists. Even Spike Milligan published a collection of not very coherent letters as *'Dear Robert, Dear Spike'*: the dust jacket describes them as 'fellow poets'. 'Am still Robert', he wrote rather desperately to an unappreciative poet friend James Reeves at the time. He did not believe he or anyone really changed. In 1961 he said, 'My personality has remained the same. . . That's the funny thing, even though externals change you stay the same person.' He also told me confidently, 'There is no time.'

Graves's most sympathetic and accurate biographer, Martin Seymour-Smith (1982, revised 1995), reads Graves's life more as a long poem than do Richard Perceval Graves (three volumes, 1986, 1990, 1995) and Miranda Seymour (1995) who read it as prose. But all three tend to judge his final years harshly, and to varying degrees all sign up to what can be called a 'received' view of Graves's life in which 'he can't be serious' about the Goddess. (Seymour-Smith signed up to a difference between inspired poetry and artificial verse, but not to the Muse.)

Graves's behaviour in his early old age caused distress to all who knew him, as well perhaps to his 'Muses.' A BBC television programme in the late 1990s without irony interviewed some of these, with the captions 'Judith Bledsoe, Muse', etc. Seymour-Smith wrote about him in the 1970s:

> Of all men living, who could be most wise
> Insists that women may put out men's eyes;
> Yet is himself protected from this ban
> On love without obedience: he can
> Inform the world that he's contented now
> In a supreme potency, and broadcast how
> He lives happy in a woman's grip—
> Ignorant he holds the hand that holds the whip....

Yet Graves took the poem in good part. Again there was the paradox of an apparent gap between his high flown and genuine belief in the Goddess, and his earthy recognition that 'the poetic faculty is atrophied in every edu-

cated person who does not privately struggle to cultivate it.' His Muses
were, after all real women. How did each contribute to Graves's vision of
the Goddess? How did 'this thing' manifest itself in them?

The first possible Muse is described in *Goodbye to All That* (1929) as
'Marjorie, a probationer nurse' at the hospital where Graves was recovering
from almost fatal wounds in 1916. This was Marjorie Machin, then aged 18
or 19. Graves wrote about her to an officer friend, 'I am quite satisfied to
find that I have the power of falling in love with a girl.' He stated in *Goodbye
to All That* that he 'felt difficulty in adjusting [him]self to the experience of
woman-love'. According to a later poem, 'A Dream of Frances Speedwell'
he had fallen in love from a distance in his teens with a friend of his sister. He
also experienced an idealistic and non-physical love for such male friends as
a fellow-officer who had been killed:

> Walking through the trees to cool my heat and pain,
> I know that David's here with me again.
> All that is simple, happy, strong he is…

Graves had to, as he saw it, reject Marjorie Machin because she was cor-
responding with another officer at the front and he had seen what happened
when such men received rejections from girl friends. This episode does not
fit in with a pseudo-Freudian myth of Graves's smooth transfer of sexuality
from public school boys and fellow officers to his 'boyish' first wife Nancy
Nicholson, and was at first denied by all three biographers. But letters from
Graves about Marjorie turned up in 1995 proving them wrong.

It is assumed that Graves wrote his first love poems to Nancy, which
appeared in his volumes *The Treasure Box* (1919) and *Country Sentiment* (1920).
But I wonder if Marjorie appears in 'Marigolds' ('marigold' and 'Marjorie'
are etymologically related) in *Fairies and Fusiliers* (1917):

> New beginnings and new shoots
> Spring again from hidden roots.
> Pull or stab or cut or burn,
> Love must ever yet return.

In the received view, Nancy was an early feminist but a scatterbrained
nitwit whose inconsistency prevented Graves from resolving his war neu-
rosis. His life with her, this view went, was at first a pastoral and domestic

escape, but she was not his intellectual equal, and after a series of friendships with guru-like men (T.E. Lawrence and a Nepalese philosopher, Basanta Malik) he found himself more than ready for the arrival of the brilliant American poet Laura Riding.

Much is made in the biographies of the fact that when Graves first met Nancy she was wearing trousers. Well, she was aged 17 at the time, and she was doing war work on a farm. But her main ambition was to have four children soon, which she did. She came from a family of painters (her father William Nicholson and her brother Ben). She had been born at Chaucer's cottage in Woodstock. She can hardly have been dim: there was a meeting of minds between her and the not unintelligent Graves. 'Nancy and I called ourselves socialists', Graves remarks in *Goodbye to All That*. They also shared feminist ideas (they gave their sons the surname Graves, the daughters Nicholson—an unusual and courageous decision) as well as a determination to live a pastoral life in the country, a tendency to take off on impulsive holidays and treks and to live beyond their means, and an absolute outspokenness and absence of class bias in their dealings with all and sundry. They set up a country grocers shop together—though it failed. She illustrated his poems and nursery rhymes for children, and worked, when she could, on her own painting. In photographs she is apple-cheeked, gangly, unaffected—an original. And wearing a dress. His poems to her—or 'through' her as the Elizabethans would have said—convey her as poignant, lovely, suffering, intense and real, never ideal. Graves never suppressed these poems, as he did those from the War: he did not see them as an 'escape'. He is supposed, in cliché, to have escaped the horrors of war with Nancy. He just fell in love with her.

> Are you shaken, are you stirred
>   By a whisper of love?
> Spellbound to a word
>   Does time cease to move,
> Till her calm grey eye
>   Expands to a sky
> And the clouds of her hair
>   Like storms go by?

But already in his earliest poems through Nancy, Graves is suffering from her anger at him:

One smile relieves
A heart that grieves
Though deadly sad it be,
And one hard look
Can close the book
That lovers love to see.

Their tragedy was that they were naïve. They thought that Robert could write poems and Nancy could paint, and they could have four children, and remain themselves. They were dirt poor and became dependent on increasingly angry families (emotionally blackmailing in the case of the Graves parents). None of Graves's books before 1929, when he was 34, sold well. Nancy may have had an affair with one of his best friends.

Then in 1926 Laura Riding arrived to live with them. They had both written to her, in America, when they came across her poems. Frances Wilson in her fascinating *Literary Seductions* has dissected famous literary relationships—Henry Miller and Anais Nin, Osip and Nadezhda Mandelstam, and Graves and Riding—which were invented in their participants' minds before they even began. Graves had already fallen in love with Riding in her poem, 'The Quids', about 'slippery monads', published in John Crowe Ransom's magazine *The Fugitive*. He and Nancy (who had also liked the poem) invited her to join them. When he met her at the boat train in London he was momentarily horrified by her over made-up appearance, but in another train, to Oxford, he saw a light about her head. As 'a Trinity' all three decided to live in a ménage à trois (here as idealistically as Shelley, whom Graves never liked, with whom the experiment was equally disastrous and fatal). God knows how this will be treated in a film due for release in 2012 about the Robert, Nancy, Laura triangle, to be titled *The Laureate*.

The First World War poet Graves admired and was influenced by most was Isaac Rosenberg—who wrote a powerful poem 'The Female God.' Rosenberg is sidelined, for some reason, in the modern revival of the Great War Poets—as Graves largely is: his war poems do not fit the bill any more than Rosenberg's—or for that matter Charles Hamilton Sorley's. They are not war poems, just poems. (The War poet of the sentimental academic / popular cult is *only* a war poet and preferably a pacifist: after the war he is either literally dead, like Owen, or poetically so, like Sassoon.)

Graves was more than ready to make Laura into the Semitic Female God prophesied by Rosenberg in his adumbrations from the Lilith of the Old Testament Apocrypha. He had already discovered the White Goddess / Muse in the years with Nancy, first in his enthusiasm for Skelton who had the name of the Muse Calliope embroidered on his robe, then in his biblical study, along Rosenberg lines, *My Head! My Head!* He was also influenced by the great psychologist William Rivers who treated 'shell-shocked' soldiers (as in the film *Regeneration*) and whose book *Instinct and Behaviour* is an under-read classic. Rivers alerted Graves to the cult of the Great Mother in some tribal societies, and to Malinowski's field research among the Trobrianders of the Pacific who existed without patriarchy (though not with matriarchy either).

Riding exerted a powerful magic over Graves and others—not least through her poignant and truthful early poems, and in her erotic presence in which he merged, perhaps for the first time, love and thought:

> To speak of the hollow nape where the close chaplet
> Of thought is bound, the loose-ends lying neat
> In two strands downward, where the shoulders open
> Casual and strong below, waiting their burden,
> And the long spine begins its downward journey:
> The hair curtains this postern silkily,
> This secret stairway by which thought will come....

She stimulated thought in him, but it is a mistake to claim, in the received view, that she originated any of his ideas. Not only was the Goddess already present in his mind, he had already come to the view that 'there is no time'. Riding's famous view that time has stopped was first expressed in the 1930s, though it may have derived earlier from Leibnitz who thought time was merely the relation among 'monads' (the 'quids'). But Graves had already asked 'Does time cease to move?' in that early poem to Nancy. He had already written a book on *The Interpretation of Dreams*, and he, and presumably Riding, read J. W. Dunne's *An Experiment with Time* (1927) which concludes that dreams consist of images about a third each from the past, present, and future. Dunne's findings were replicated in a series of meticulous experiments by Krippner and Ullman in New York, 1966–1969. Intellectuals in the late 1920s were preoccupied with notions of time. Wyndham Lewis's *Time and Western Man*, 1927, describes this as a 'time cult'. And quantum physics was getting underway. In his history of the period (with Alan Hodge), *The Long Weekend*, Graves referred to 'time's ineluctable wibble-wobble'. In *The White Goddess* he declared his faith in 'more-than-coincidence.' Riding had not started this train of thought in Graves, but she exemplified it:

If strange things happen where she is,
So that men say that graves open
And the dead walk, or that futurity
Becomes a womb and the unborn are shed,
Such portents are not to be wondered at,
Being tourbillions in Time made
By the strong pulling of her bladed mind
Through that ever-reluctant element.

Riding's bladed mind did open Graves up. When the dust settled after
her famous suicide leap from a fourth floor window—as she later said, 'It
was the shortest way out of the room' where she, Graves, Nancy, and an
Anglo-Irishman called Phibbs whom Riding wished to coopt into a new
'Four' had been arguing—Graves and she went to Mallorca. Nancy lived
for many years with Phibbs. Although named 'the Devil' by Riding, with
Graves's acquiescence Phibbs was a good father substitute to the children.

'The Fall' broke Riding's pelvis and back, left her partly crippled, and
provided her with a reason for an abrupt change. As Joyce Wexler remarks,
'She treated her fall as an act of will that had allowed her to shed her personal identity and enter a universal state of being', and she would speak
of having died—a leaf, surely, out of Graves's book: he had 'died' in 1916
when wounded by a shell fragment, set aside for dead, and having his obitu-
ary published in *The Times* which later had to rescind it.

She announced that 'bodies have had their day', and she put this into
practice. She had already written an essay about sex, 'The Damned Thing.'
When she and Graves moved to Mallorca (following a tip by Gertrude Stein:
'it's Paradise, if you can stand it') they were occasional lovers, but she had
stopped this by 1933. Or not technically: she would let him come into her
bedroom to comfort her during thunderstorms, and she would 'relieve' him
from time to time—if he was 'good'; an effective process known to behav-
iourists as intermittent reinforcement.

A paradox is that this man who did not believe in time made his living
writing the best *historical* novels of the 20th century. Although of course he
offhandedly rejected history, agreeing with Laura Riding that 'Geography
is about maps, history about chaps.' He let some of his feelings through in
I Claudius (which Riding dismissed as a pot-boiler though they lived off its
proceeds: she literally tore to shreds a pile of favourable reviews) where
a source of evil is Augustus's wife LIVIA—perhaps by more-than-coinci-

dence containing 3 of the same letters, given the Latin equivalence of V and
U, as LAURA.

After the 'Fall' Riding's poems were never the same: they lacked feeling.
I suspect she had suffered brain damage. Even without direct impact to the
head, in an impact severe enough to break so many bones the brain is shaken
about, the frontal lobes being particularly vulnerable. A common 'frontal'
effect is a certain disconnection between thought and feeling (although it
may remit with time). As if in conformity with Riding, it became difficult
for Graves to admit feeling to his poems. Although the received version is
that Riding inspired Graves to his best poetry, and he did dutifully write a
poem to her as 'The Sovereign Muse', his poems of the 1930s are mainly dry
records of depression:

> Trudge, body, and climb, trudge and climb,
> But not to stand again on any peak of time:
> Trudge, body.....
>
> Before each sun may rise, you salute it for set:
> Trudge, body.

Riding occasionally set him up with passing women so that he could grat-
ify what she saw as his brutish urges, but sent them packing if he showed any
signs of attachment—more intermittent reinforcement.

Riding's role, psychologically, in Graves's life was less to inspire him than
to punish him. He later remarked to Seymour-Smith 'I treated Nancy badly
and my punishment was Laura.' Riding was more like his mother Amahlia
Ranke—originally German speaking even, puritanical, righteous—than
any other woman in his life. And since, after all, a man doesn't usually sleep
with his mother, the eventually celibate partnership was appropriate.

In its early days, when they loved each other, before the Fall, their relationship was good for each other's work. Graves much valued and frequently quoted Riding's phrase (in a poem to him): 'Forgive me, giver, if I
destroy the gift: it is so nearly what would please me. I cannot but perfect
it.' Poet-critic couples can be productive—I'm thinking of the Catalan poet
and painter Narcis Comadira whose wife Dolors Oller is a literary critic—
but Riding's view was particularly harsh: 'the female mind is the judge, and
the male mind the subject of judgment... But the male mind has now had
all the time there is for working up case.' She also wrote that 'criticism is
death.' She certainly didn't accept it for herself.

There is no space here to discuss the famous break up between Graves and Riding. 'She ran off with a man called Schuyler', Graves summarised to me at Oxford while warmly recommending I read her poems. Events in New Hope, Pennsylvania in 1939, when Riding famously announced after her decade of celibacy 'Schuyler and I do', were more complex. Miranda Seymour has even written a novel about this drama, *The Telling*. Riding had embraced time literally in the person of Schuyler Jackson, a charming mediocrity of whom she expected great things: he had reviewed her poetry favourably in *Time* (yes, time) magazine, calling her collection 'the book of books of the mid-twentieth century.' But she 'renounced' poetry (which had dried up anyway) in favour of work on *An Exact Dictionary of Meanings*—originally to have been assisted by Graves, but transposed into a collaboration with Jackson. This turns out (it was published in 1997, six years after her death) to reveal the late Riding as an Aristotelian essentialist of the most banal sort: words are 'precious essences of human perception' and language is 'the essential moral meeting ground'—whereas in her early days it was 'a form of laziness.'

The first act of the New Hope drama had in fact been played out in Brittany earlier that year. While Riding and Jackson were gearing up (à la *Literary Seductions*) by transatlantic correspondence for their future union, Graves started a relationship with Beryl, wife of his friend Alan Hodge. His poetry suddenly came to a new life:

> Lovers in the act dispense
> With such meum-tuum sense
> As might warningly reveal
> What they must not pick or steal,
> And their nostrum is to say:
> 'I and you are both away.'
>
> After, when they disentwine
> You from me and yours from mine....

'The Thieves' resonates with a four way theft: on the surface each lover steals the other, but in the light of the history each is stealing the other from another—Hodge and Riding. I wonder how much Riding's fury at this drove her to 'do' with Jackson? At any rate her fury with Graves endured. As late as 1983 she wrote in a letter to *The London Review of Books* that 'Graves was, in his basic instincts, a lout.'

In the received view Beryl is the subject of many of Graves's most tender love poems, but was basically 'ordinary', a relief from the exacting Riding, and a domestic wife and mother ('splendid Beryl!') who meekly accepted Graves's establishment of the doctrine that the Muse is 'the perpetual other woman' and stood by while he fell in love with a series of young bimbo Muses. She has received a bad press from some of Graves's so called friends. (Similarly, Sassoon had disparaged Nancy). The American journalist and editor of *Time* Tom Matthews described Beryl, who was strikingly good-looking, as looking like a drowned cat, and trying to 'be like Laura' in berating Graves, before she found her real vocation as a wife and mother. James Reeves as he deteriorated in late middle age used to rail on about how Beryl 'was waiting for Robert at the boat'; in fact, he returned from America before she did. The two of Graves's poet friends who at their best could match his level in poetry, Norman Cameron and Martin Seymour-Smith, liked her. Seymour-Smith's account of the Graves-Beryl relationship is attentive and balanced: he thought Graves's poems to Beryl his best because 'to a real woman':

> Now that I love you, now that I recall
> All scattered elements of will that swooped
> By night as jealous dreams through windows
> To circle above the beds like bats,
> Or as dawn-birds flew blindly at the panes
> In curiosity rattling out their brains—
>
> Now that I love you, as not before,
> Now you can be and say, as not before:
> The mind clears and the heart true-mirrors you
> Where at my side an early watch you keep
> And all self-bruising heads loll into sleep.

Beryl could 'be and say', all right. She remarked to my wife and me in her old age, 'I don't like myths very much: they're usually dead. Though of course, as Robert would say, they can also be alive. The myth of Money, for instance.' This is real talk—and what Graves liked in those close to him. He wrote in another poem of their 'honest first reluctance to agree', though others 'may flatter me with absolute agreement.'

In 1948 Graves published *The White Goddess*—the first of a series of controversial books including *Greek Myths* and *The Nazarene Gospel Restored* in which he offered a Goddess-centred interpretation of myth and religion. Seymour-Smith, having read widely in the anthropology of the early twentieth century shows scepticism about this interpretation. But more recent work by the archaeologist Maria Gimbutas on the goddess-centred religion of 'Old Europe' supports it. In areas where I have some knowledge, for example in Irish literature and tree lore, Graves is invariably accurate, although some of his archaeological evidence at second hand is not. He is as ever down to earth, simultaneously old-fashioned and up to date:

> The function of poetry is religious invocation of the Muse; its use is the experience of mixed exaltation and horror that her presence excites. But 'nowadays'? Function and use remain the same: only the application has changed. This was once a warning to man that he must keep in harmony with the family of living creatures among which he was born, by obedience to the wishes of the lady of the house; it is now a reminder that he has disregarded the warning, turned the house upside down by capricious experiments in philosophy, science and industry, and brought ruin on himself and his family.

There were four later 'Muses'. The first was Judith Bledsoe who was aged 17 in 1950 when she first arrived in Mallorca and fulfilled, uncannily as Graves saw it, the role of the Goddess. Graves was then 55 and Beryl 35. Judith was beautiful, a not incapable painter, and became friends with Beryl. However, Graves took a fussy and proprietary interest in her love affairs, and suffered genuinely at her inevitable betrayal of his expectations when she became engaged to a man memorably described in Graves's poem 'The Bluefly'. His poems 'through' Judith are sometimes formulaic. A few are among his best. 'The Window Sill' ends as, apparently, their love did:

> Julia, leaning on her window sill.
> 'I love you still,'
> She said, 'O love me still!'
>
> I answered: 'Julia, do you love me best?'
> 'What of this breast,'
> She mourned, 'this flowery breast?'

Then a wild sobbing spread from door to door,
And every floor
Cried shame on every floor,

As she unlaced her bosom to disclose
Each breast a rose,
A white and cankered rose.

After a gap of several years (during which the Graves's last child was born), the second Muse, Margot Callas, appeared in 1959. Perhaps this would have been another 'miraculous, unpredictable and unassessable event in non-history' (as he later defined poems to Seymour-Smith): Graves did not want to have a 'vulgar' affair with any of his Muses. He did want to be free to record, as a poet, along the lines he had set out in *The White Goddess*, the truth about any woman he loved. He did fall in love with each of the four Muses. And why not? So far as is known, Beryl did not object: indeed she left Graves to follow his own judgment—which was all right insofar as this judgment remained intact. And he always lived his life openly: it would be hard to imagine him having a secret mistress. There does, however, seem to have been a disturbance of the sexual relationship between Graves and Beryl in the late 1950s.

The complicating factor was not so much Margot herself (she too remained friends with Beryl) as the involvement of a 'rival' in the form of Alastair Reid, a Scot who made his living as a teacher of poetry in an expensive u.s. junior college for young women, as a translator from poets in Spanish, and as a writer of articles for *The New Yorker*. He turned up in Mallorca (by then a lot of people were turning up) and after a period of study of Graves from a distance moved in to become his bosom friend. They even became blood brothers by mixing bloods from cut fingers. How the author of *The White Goddess* became close friends with the author of a volume of verse called *Oddments, Inklings, Omens, Moments* is a mystery. And Graves's dogged insistence on being himself (whatever that turned out to be) was at odds with Reid's eventual view that we consist of various 'separate selves.' But Graves seems to have needed a male friend in Mallorca: his old friends Matthews, James Reeves and Seymour-Smith could seldom visit, and Norman Cameron had died.

Reid and Margot inevitably ran off together. Just as inevitably, they soon separated. Reid was diabolised by Graves, rather as Phibbs had been by Riding in 1928. He became part of *The White Goddess* triangle formula into which many of Graves's poems to Margot were beginning to fit: Goddess as lover and betrayer, faithful poet, and diabolical rival.

Apparently Graves was worried after his prostate operation of 1959 that he might be impotent, and Margot seems to have fixed this. (It is reported, though, that their relationship was 'only occasionally physical'.) The 'bloody horrible' poem 'Lion Lover' is about her, as is 'The Death Grapple':

> Lying between your sheets, I challenge
> A watersnake in a swoln cataract
> Or a starved lioness among drifts of snow.
>
> Yet dare it out, for after each death grapple,
> Each gorgon stare borrowed from very hate,
> A childish innocent smile touches your lips,
> Your eyelids droop, fearless and careless,
> And sleep remoulds the lineaments of love.

'There's always masochism in love', Graves remarked to me around that time, at Oxford. Unfortunately the next Muse put this to the test in a less lovely way. This was Cindy Lee, aka Aemilia Laraçuen, aka finally Emilia MacKinley, but generally known as Cindy. With her it was certainly physical, as she revealed in a kiss-and-tell article for *The Sunday Times* in 2006. And for once Graves seems out of his depth, his language inadequate to what he is living, as in 'The Blow.'

> You struck me on the face and I, who strike
> Only to kill, stood in confusion like
> Death's fool. Your ugly blow
> Had fallen soft as snow.
>
> Love me for what I am, with liberty
> To curb my rage; I love you for what will be—
> Your urgent sun—
> Therefore acquitting you of error.
>
> Laughter becomes us: gift of the third eye
> That passes nothing by.

The first two stanzas are more than up to the event, especially the old soldier's acknowledgment 'I who strike / Only to kill', then the final couplet becomes almost a nostrum—a way out. Still, Graves achieved a total clarity in some of his poems to Cindy:

'This year she has changed greatly'—meaning you—
My sanguine friends agree,
And hope thereby to reassure me.

No, child, you never change; neither do I.
Indeed all our lives long
We are still fated to do wrong...

Graves's experiencing with Cindy what he referred to as 'the blood sports of desire' and his pouring out of money to her did make Beryl suffer. According to William Graves she used to sit silently for long periods holding her head. Later, more cheerfully, she described Cindy as 'the only disaster Muse'. Graves might actually have left Mallorca, and stayed in Mexico where at one point he followed Cindy, but luckily for him she ran off one time too many with another man, the beat 'poet' Howard Hart, and he returned home a more or less shattered man. But was Graves really 'the hand that holds the whip'? The various Muses were surely just being themselves. Seymour-Smith wrote that 'the essential cruelty of women is not really a good lesson for a poet to teach' and that Graves 'turned into a bigot who assumed that women were cruel in their essence—just because (or so it seemed) a notoriously self-regarding woman [Riding] had been cruel to him.' But Seymour-Smith himself wrote the alarming poem sequence 'Reminiscences of Norma' about the incidental cruelty of a woman's part-indifference. (Graves commiserated with him about it.) Perhaps women, at least when not constrained or bullied by a patriarchal society, are cruel to men in their inevitable disappointment in them. And the war between the sexes goes back a long way. Think of Catullus: 'Odi et amo. Et excrucior'—roughly translatable as: 'I hate and I love. And it hurts like hell...'

Besides which, leaving aside the more programmatic aspects of the White Goddess's—or indeed nature's—cruelty, Graves's poems, as much as Seymour-Smith's, are often about tenderness and gratitude to women.

After Cindy the pieces were picked up, essentially, by Beryl. Graves eventually recovered his sense of humour and wrote a poem about how some of his friends 'plucked him like a fowl.'

Then the last Muse turned up in the person of Juli Simons (now Julia Simonne) the daughter of old friends, who in 1966 at the age of 17 visited him in a London hospital and told him she had fallen in love with him. According to Seymour-Smith 'everyone gave a huge sigh of relief when she came along.'

Although Seymour-Smith's view that 'he holds the hand that holds the whip' underestimates the character of the various 'Muses', Graves's late poems can be formulaic. As Seymour-Smith puts it, he was 'dutiful to the course of his love as prescribed by his own theories'. But still miraculous poems occur. Here is a short one from 1967 when he was aged 72, 'Green Flash':

> Watch now for a green flash, for the last moment
> When the sun plunges into sea;
> And breathe no wish (most wishes are of weakness)
> When green, Love's own heraldic tincture,
> Leads in the mystagogues of Mother Night:
> Owls, planets, dark oracular dreams.
> Nightfall is not mere failure of daylight.

Graves suffered from mild cognitive impairment, not dementia, starting around 1970—not earlier. He had become muddled on the BBC TV progamme *The Brains Trust* in 1960 or so, and around the same time the journalist Philip Toynbee maliciously described him as 'in his anecdotage'. But at least since 1918 he had been capable of what he called 'sudden abstraction' in the form of absent mindedness and even occasional aphasia: he wrote in a poem about his 'unfinished sentences.' Until 1974 or so his letters were as always, and his poems were lucid. Eventually he developed dementia. This has been diagnosed, gratuitously, by Spike Milligan and Dr Anthony Clare, who is not known to have met or treated him, as Alzheimer's Disease. But his early cognitive impairment was almost certainly not Alzheimer's; if it was, it was one of the longest cases on record since Alzheimer's lasts five to fifteen years from its first signs and he did not die until 1985; further, unlike Alzheimer's it was characterised by lapses in concentration, not in memory. Furthermore, in the 'petrified self' (as the neuropsychologist Robin Morris terms it) of Alzheimer's there is limited capacity for insight ('My memory's fine'), whereas in the 1970s Graves was agonised by awareness of failing memory.

Most likely his eventual dementia was 'mixed'—the cumulative result of episodes of anoxia—severe loss of blood and near-death when wounded in 1916; a fall downstairs when recovering from his wounds, in which he lacerated his head; a botched nose operation in 1917; a history of boxing at school and of possible head injury (broken nose) playing rugby; a probable concussion from his jump from a third floor window in 1928 (he was unconscious and twitching when Phibbs arrived on the scene); the necessity for scores of blood transfusions after the prostate operation in 1959 which revealed he lacked a blood clotting factor; a serious nose operation in 1971 which required unusually heavy doses of anaesthetic and after which he complained of memory loss; a sinus operation in 1972; an unspecified head injury in a car crash in Mexico which nonetheless made him ill for weeks; and finally the kind of decay associated with Alzheimer's Disease. Graves was a warrior. According to Seymour-Smith (in conversation) even in Graves's middle age if he took off his shirt to do gardening, his 1916 wound scar could be seen to ooze.

In his last years he agonised about having killed Germans, got into a fight with a German in Deia and began speaking German as he had in summers as a child. He wandered restlessly and got lost. He told an old friend, Honor Wyatt: 'I am in hell.' He stopped speaking after 1980. His death and funeral are lovingly described in the memoirs of William and Lucia Graves.

'Strange things happen where she is', Graves wrote of Laura Riding. Possibly strange things happen where *anyone* is, but Graves chose to notice them with his Muses. As Hardy wrote of himself: 'He was one who noticed such things.' As Seymour-Smith has pointed out, the character of the woman who inspires a male poet comes across in the poems. Graves trusted Julia Simonne:

> With you for mast and sail and flag,
> And anchor never known to drag,
> Death's narrow but oppressive sea
> Looks not unnavigable to me.

He wrote far too many poems to her, as she generously acknowledged in a 2007 article for the journal *Gravesiana*, pointing out that he ran out of time to subject his late poems to the pruning he had made of earlier ones. Most of them show a loss of intensity and a weakening of his rhythm towards prose. But they are often surprisingly thoughtful. Simonne's presence (or absence: they were usually apart) allowed the aging and often rambling Graves to explore his wilder ideas about magic, the fourth dimension—time—and the 'fifth dimensional' events that transcend it. In her article she quotes a letter he wrote to her on the 20th of April, 1970:

> I am the expression of a combination of genes, which I chose myself. Reincarnation...would mean a different set of genes and inherited memories. If I am then asked, 'Then at what time did you take these decisions about yourself?' I answer 'Time is a convenience, not a fixed irreversible flow, which man is capable of disregarding (in the sense of fixed fated occurrence).... From the point of distant stars, I will not be born for millions of light-years; but I have my fixed place in the universe and this can never be altered. If therefore I am asked, 'When did you decide on your birth?' I answer: 'In the moment of death, when alone I have a full conspectus of my life, which is a sort of capsule containing an endless circle, head swallowing tail.

Crazy stuff! Must be dementia! But this harks back to his experience of near-death in 1916 and to his ideas on time in the 1920s. He had written a brilliant though hostile essay on Nietzsche in 1935, and he is here referring to Nietzsche's theory of 'eternal recurrence' and 'amor fatis', namely that we live exactly the same lives again and again and wisdom consists of loving our fate—i.e. our eternal recurrence. Graves is also referring to the neo-Platonic image of eternity, the 'dracon ouroboros'—the serpent eating its own tail. And he is anticipating a cosmological theory of the 21st century: that time does not exist. In *The End of Time* (1999) the theoretical physicist Julian Barbour sets this theory out, and currently he and his research group are working on the mathematics of a minimalist universe of space in which time is not necessary. Barbour's theory of why we *experience* time is that the universe contains 'time capsules', defined as 'any fixed pattern that creates or encodes the appearance of motion, change or history.' And 'the mature brain is a time capsule. History resides in its structure.'

By more-than-coincidence, Barbour's father Neville was a school friend of Graves. But I know from Barbour that he is not aware of Graves's (or Riding's) view of time, and certainly not of Graves's definition of 'a sort of capsule containing an endless circle'—and of course Barbour's matching view post-dates 1970 so Graves could not have known it.

John Donne described his first meeting of his Muse Ann More as a 'strange and fatal interview.' Graves's fate (like that of many poets in a very long tradition) was revealed to him by those women he saw as possessed by the Muse, or the Goddess, around whom the events of more-than-coincidence occurred—culminating spontaneously in poems. His poems are no more under his own control than Fate—who in mythology is above all gods and goddesses in a timeless universe. Poems are born of Chance and Necessity (to use the physicist Jacques Monod's equivalent to fate). 'This thing' is both inspiration and what it records. Poems are one offs, 'miraculous events in non-history', whereas physics is a deliberate research programme which requires replicability. But both physics and poetry reveal that the universe is a stranger place than common sense allows. 'He can't mean it.' Oh yes he can.

Robert Selby

Splendour

Sunlight makes the beech hedge glow,
so too the bulbous, pink tulips below
the kitchen window at which we
spread apricot jam from a shining jar
onto buttered brown toast. The kitchen is host
to May light, spick and span on spoon and pan.
I try the tea. It is hot but sugarless,
unsatisfactory, and I recall
my grandfather's refrain down the hall
if his was unsweetened by sugar
or, in later years, *Splenda*—
you did not have to be in the same room
to see him eyeing his cup with a feigned frown—
'Has the sugar boat gone down?'

Anne Stevenson

A Visit

In a dream you came to me
just as you used to be,
cocky, handsome,
smooth without a beard,
though hardly self-assured
as you appeared,
having, as you confessed,
lost all your money.

Somewhere on my messy desk
were the intimate records
of our joint income.
Yes, here was a file
of tattered yellow strips
heaped neatly next to me,
morphing into the Chance pile
in Monopoly.
And here was the boot,
the lovely Lagonda, the hat,
the luxury liner.
Why did I always choose the boot,
and you the boat or the car?
And how had these cards
cut out for clever children
turned into paying-in-slips?
I stared at the lucky million
printed in Ariel Bold
on every one.

'Just as I thought' I said,
'You're rich!' 'No, just old'—
lightly admitted,
as rueful, maybe surprised,
you shook your head.

I woke up when I realized
that every delectable moment
your daring had won you
or earned you had been well spent.
You weren't unhappy, dead.

A Match

Lashing her matchbox with a match, he freed a golden flame
To light her cigarette before his, like a gentleman.
It was their champagne-sipping wedding night, but all the same
He put the match back in the box—it was his party game—
Quipping, 'That was a good one. Let's save it to use again.'

Rory Waterman

Reverdie

The broadened buzzard
glides in an orbit,
as if on a wire,
then twists, breaking free;

a bee revs its engine
and limps from stamen
to stamen, then lifts,
chicanes to the trees.

Your gaze follows one,
mine the other;
they mingle silently
in the thickening canopy.

Dana Gioia

The Argument

After you put the phone down,
The words don't vanish all at once.
They linger in the wires and circuitry,
Pushing their way through the noisy
Crowds of other conversations,
Still trying to provoke a response.

Endlessly repeating themselves,
They want to argue out
Their side of things—furious
That not one syllable will listen.

So angry they hardly notice
How much weaker they become
Each time they speak.
Until at last they huddle
As whispers in the long
Black tunnel of their saying.

But see how strong they are today.
Listen to them rage above the quiet road,
Screeching out their righteousness
Along the miles of tight-strung wire.

Antonio Machado

Traveler

Traveler, your footsteps are
the road, there's nothing more;
traveler, there is no road,
the road is made by walking.
Walking makes the road,
and if you turn around,
you only see the path
you cannot walk again.
Traveler, there is no road,
only a track of foam upon the sea.

—translated by Dana Gioia

Marcia Menter

The Accessibility of Anthony Hecht

IN A SEEMINGLY GLOWING REVIEW of Anthony Hecht's final book, a collection of critical essays called *Melodies Unheard* (*Poetry* Magazine, January
2004), Jon Mooallem began by praising the poet's astonishing breadth and
depth of learning, citing references within a single essay to 'Herodotus,
Stephen Sondheim, contemporary photography, Ruskin … Le Goff, Freud
… Elizabethan lyrics, Martin Luther's musical compositions (which Hecht
notates) … the 1811 edition of the *Dictionary of the Vulgar Tongue*, and even
a cameo by Paul Tibbets Jr., group commander of the *Enola Gay*….' (Yep,
that's Hecht, in all his polymath glory.) Such 'expansive allusiveness,' far
from being tedious or gratuitous, Mooallem wrote, 'is always employed in
the service of a specific and inventive argument.'

Mooallem went on in this mostly laudatory, gee-whiz vein for three
more pages before wheeling in for the kill: 'Yet as well-informed and deft
a performance as it is, it would be impossible to discuss *Melodies Unheard*
without addressing the question of its relevance. … Like Hecht's poetry,
the prose here is cogently and artfully written; it is brilliant. It is *not*, however, stylistically inviting or even particularly current. … There's a certain
gentility that's hard to penetrate. …[W]ith so much to say of value for any
reader of poetry, what a shame he could not meet a broader, less specialized
audience at least half way.'

I remember reading this review with my mouth open, not just because
this young journalistic Turk was mothballing a great, still-living poet-critic,
but also because Mooallem clearly assumed that Hecht's aggressive erudition
and intellectual dexterity were virtues of the past: 'His writing … reveals
him as a certain type of post-war literary fellow.'

Well, yes. Yes it does. Hecht is that type of post-war literary fellow
who has experienced first-hand the horrors of his time and processed those
experiences with extraordinary decency and humanity. J. D. McClatchy,
editor of the new volume of Hecht's *Selected Poems* (Borzoi Poetry, $17.95),
speaks in his introduction of the *nobility* of Hecht's work: 'high, important
matters dealt with in a manner that is contained, dignified and open, full of
feeling.' Hecht is sometimes lofty but never genteel. He invites the reader
to know more, see more and understand more. He believes we can keep up
with him if we try. He demands repeated readings, each of which shows us
something crucial we didn't see before. In the mirrored, exquisitely crafted

Anthony Hecht Selected Poems, edited by J. D. McClatchy. Alfred A. Knopf, 2011. 288pp., $17.95 U.S.A., $20.50 Canada pbk

surfaces of his poems, he reveals himself as a Great Soul in the context of a hellish century.

I don't know if Hecht saw Mooallem's review—he died of lymphoma later that year, at 81—but I'm sure it wouldn't have surprised him. In an indispensable book-length interview with Philip Hoy (1999), Hecht bemoaned the 'tragic' change in English Departments throughout the U.S., which, he said, had broken up 'into embattled, intransigent factions demanding exclusive allegiance on behalf of their own mostly ideological agendas: feminism, black studies, gay studies, prison literature, deconstruction ... [T]hese days very few who teach at the college and university level are devoted to literature for its own sake, and deeply acquainted with it.' Hecht, by contrast, came of age during the flowering of the New Criticism, which encouraged subtlety, irony and wit. He apprenticed himself to teachers who challenged him to read widely and think deeply, including John Crowe Ransom (who actually coined the term 'New Criticism'). He often disagreed with Ransom, he told Hoy, 'without losing any respect for him.... For one learned from him, not facts or positions, but a posture of the mind and spirit ... And one learned to pay keen attention to poetic detail.' Hecht later learned by adopting other models, including Yeats (who, he says, served as 'a sort of Zen master'), Frost, Eliot, Stevens and Auden. He came by his craft honestly, though a lifetime of passionate study.

So one should not pick up the Hecht *Selected* expecting to catch every obscure reference and applaud every felicity of form. One should pick him up for pleasure: the pleasure of language at the highest level, the pleasure of new connections lighting up the brain, and definitely the pleasure of disagreeing with him—without losing an iota of respect. There is also the unexpected pleasure (if I may call it that) of watching Hecht disprove Theodor Adorno's famous, fatuous assertion that 'to write poetry after Auschwitz is barbaric.' Hecht brings us face to face with the Holocaust without sparing or absolving us, yet, as McClatchy points out, we are uplifted by his enormous dignity.

I heard Hecht read his late sestina 'The Book of Yolek' at West Chester some years ago. It was my first encounter with his work, and it blew me away. It opens, as many Hecht poems do, in the middle of a place and situation where you can't immediately get your bearings:

> The dowsed coals fume and hiss after your meal
> Of grilled brook trout, and you saunter off for a walk
> Down the fern trail, it doesn't matter where to,

Just so you're weeks and worlds away from home,
And among midsummer hills have set up camp
In the deep bronze glories of declining day.

It's as pastoral as Frost, especially the bit about sauntering, though you've
noticed nervously that the poem has a German epigraph, which McClatchy's
note in the *Selected* identifies as Martin Luther's rendering of John 19:7 but,
annoyingly, does not translate: 'We have a law / And by that law he must
die.' Stanza two darkens the picture a bit: 'You remember, peacefully, an
earlier day / In childhood … That summer you got lost on a Nature Walk…'
And then comes stanza three:

The fifth of August, 1942.
It was morning and very hot. It was the day
They came at dawn with rifles to The Home
For Jewish Children, cutting short the meal
Of bread and soup, lining them to walk
In close formation off to a special camp.

The poem is based on a true account of Polish orphans being marched
off to a death camp, among them a five-year-old boy named Yolek, but
it is equally about the unnamed 'you' in stanza one, who is obsessed with
the story:

Whether on a silent, solitary walk
Or among crowds, far off or safe at home,
You will remember, helplessly, that day,
And the smell of the smoke, and the loudspeakers of the camp.
Wherever you are, Yolek will be there too.

Hecht told Hoy that the persistent end-word repetition of the sestina
form 'seemed to lend itself especially well to a topic felt obsessively.' I'd call
that a major understatement. This is the best sestina I know of in English;
it's as though the form were created for the content. (I find most sestinas so
labored that my eyes start rolling back in my head by the third or fourth
stanza.) 'Prepare to receive him in your home some day,' says the poem's
last passage. 'He will walk in as you're sitting down to a meal.' Any Jew will
automatically register this as a reference to the prophet Elijah, for whom a
place is set at the Passover Seder. Elijah is supposed to announce the coming

of the Messiah—who is also referred to, from quite a different perspective, in the poem's New Testament epigraph. This poem, complex and multi-layered yet utterly clear, could only have been written by Hecht, from the perspective of his later years.

HECHT WAS 22 IN APRIL, 1945, when his infantry division liberated the Flossenburg concentration camp, an annex of Buchenwald. Since he spoke some French and German, he was assigned to interview French prisoners to gather evidence against those who ran the camp. 'The place, the suffering, the prisoners' accounts were beyond comprehension,' Hecht told Hoy. 'For years after I would wake shrieking.' It's important to understand that even before this experience, Hecht was carrying around a habitual shame at being a Jew. Born in 1923 in New York City to parents of German-Jewish descent, he grew up in a culture where anti-Semitism was the norm, even among poets Hecht came to admire.

A further distinction needs to be made here. Many German Jews, in Germany and abroad, were assimilated into the greater culture, or at least thought they were. Reform Judaism, with prayers in the vernacular rather than in Hebrew, began in Germany and was an expression of this assimilation. Hitler's persecution came as a double shock to Jews who thought of themselves as Germans first. The Yiddish-speaking Jews of Russia and Poland, on the other hand, kept themselves separate and were routinely persecuted; German Jews viewed them with contempt. Hecht's particular brand of shame was the German-Jewish kind, where one is expected both to succeed brilliantly in the world and to be hated behind one's back for it. His brand of scholarship is also the German-Jewish kind, liberal and wide-ranging (I'm trying not to say 'catholic'). His deep familiarity with Goethe, Bach's liturgical works, Luther and the King James Bible is not surprising; neither is his desire to excel within the Academy. Samuel Menashe, who taught at Bard College with Hecht for about ten minutes, had parents who were well-educated Russian Jews, and his stance towards academia and the world at large was much more that of the Russian outsider. Both men were shattered by their wartime experiences.

Hecht was a depressive sort long before the war. In a 1988 *Paris Review* interview with McClatchy, he described a toxic childhood environment where he 'was inevitably weighed and found wanting. And a child who is told he is not good at anything is likely sooner or later to give in to a mood of defeat.' His parents subjected him to lengthy aptitude tests which, they told him, revealed he had no aptitude for anything at all. His father failed

repeatedly at business, going bankrupt and attempting suicide three times—
to the utter contempt of his mother, whose family bailed him out each time.
His younger brother (who grew up to be the poet Roger Hecht) had undi-
agnosed epilepsy and other physical problems that created still more anxiety
in the household. Hecht was eventually able to spin his childhood anguish
into poems, fairly literally in 'Apprehensions' and more obliquely in 'The
Venetian Vespers' (both of which feature spectacular descriptions of soul-
cleansing thunderstorms). But that was much later, after years of therapy
following what used to be called a nervous breakdown—a falling-apart and
pasting-back-together which I suppose is another hallmark of the post-war
literary fellow.

Hecht's first act on returning from the war was to drink himself into a
stupor for two weeks. His second was to plunge into poetry. The G.I. Bill
entitled him to resume his education, and he elected to work with Ransom,
whose influence is evident in a few of his early poems. But the big thing Hecht
learned from Ransom was the futility of trying to express strong emotions
while they're still raw: 'Instead of writing about what left me almost word-
less with confused feelings, I could write about situations that no longer dis-
turbed me, from which I had emerged either scathed or unscathed,' Hecht
told McClatchy. He could also concentrate on his craft, achieving a level of
technical mastery attained by few poets before and hardly any since.

Hecht waited until he was 31 before publishing his first collection, *A
Summoning of Stones*, in 1954. McClatchy includes seven of its thirty poems
in the *Selected*. They're gorgeous without question, and breathtakingly
erudite. They also maintain an ironic detachment that makes them easy to
admire but hard to love. For me, the strongest feeling they evoked was a
giddiness at being able to (almost) keep up with him. McClatchy provides
helpful notes in back, but these are just a starting point; it takes Google and
a broadband connection to pursue Hecht's myriad references, which make
the poems light up like a pinball machine. But here's the thing: practically
everyone has internet access now. Studying these poems may have required a
large reference library in 1954, but certainly not today.

Still, they can be daunting. In 'The Gardens of the Villa D'Este', for
example, one is confronted with seventeen eight-line stanzas swimming
down the page like goldfish. As so often with Hecht, I found myself thinking, *Sweet Tapdancing Jesus, how does he make something so complicated look so
easy?* The stanzas' halves mirror each other: the rhyme scheme is ABCDDCBA,
and the lines have three stresses, then four, five, six, six, five, four and three
again. The subject is sex.

This is Italian. Here
 Is cause for the undiminished bounce
 Of sex, cause for the lark, the animal spirit
To rise, aerated, but not beyond our reach, to spread
Friction upon the air, cause to sing loud for the bed
 Of jonquils, the linen bed, and established merit
 Of love, and grandly to pronounce
  Pleasure without peer.

It's Cole Porter with a PhD. Hecht has said he modeled this poem on
Auden's essay poems (such as 'In Praise of Limestone') which present a topic
'and wander through it in no specified order but in a casual amble,' and
that the expanding stanzas gave him room to improvise and digress. The
poem does wander, charmingly, not just through the 16th Century terraced
gardens with their ingeniously engineered cascading fountains, but through
centuries of amorous dalliance: '…White / Ejaculations leap to teach / how
fertile are these nozzles; the streams run / Góngora through the gardens,
channel themselves, and pass / To lily-padded ease, where insubordinate lass
/ And lad can cool their better parts…'

It's witty, but rather fussy and removed. So is 'Alceste in the Wilderness,'
a meditation on Moliere's *Le Misanthrope*, which sent me straight to the
internet to learn enough about the play to understand the poem. There,
interestingly, I found the poem's original published version, from *Poetry*
magazine in 1950, where it begins

Evening is clogged with gnats as the light falls
And branches bloom with gold and copper screams
Of birds with fancy prices on their tails …

By 1954, Hecht has changed line three to read:

Of birds with figured and sought-after tails

He's gotten rid of the welcome bit of cheekiness and replaced it with something stilted and lifeless, a mistake of youthful carefulness. The poem as a
whole is a vivid and ironic portrait of a fastidious mind in a corruptible body.

McClatchy includes two poems from *Summoning* that tiptoe in the direction of Hecht's wartime experiences. 'Japan' has a restraint and artifice that
serve him well in describing his impressions of that vanquished country,

where he worked in public relations for a few months after the surrender. 'Christmas Is Coming,' in blank pentameter, attempts to relate the experiences of a freezing infantryman to the old nursery rhyme. In it, Hecht told Hoy, 'the war has been curiously sanitized by being treated as an allegory.' I thought it was pretty good when I first read it. But then I came to Hecht's second collection.

The Hard Hours came out in 1967, thirteen years after *A Summoning of Stones*. McClatchy includes fourteen of its thirty-one poems. Of the seven books represented in the Selected, this is the one I feel I must own. Not because it won Hecht a Pulitzer—who cares?—but because it seems as essential to Twentieth Century poetry as Eliot's *Four Quartets*. (Hecht's books are still in print, in two volumes of *Collected Earlier Poems* and *Collected Later Poems*.) In *The Hard Hours*, Hecht retains his elegance but drops the artifice. We meet the man who witnessed the Holocaust and the poet who has acquired the skill to write about it. We also meet the man who has been forced to face his own demons.

Following the end of Hecht's first, unhappy marriage, his ex-wife remarried (in 1962) and moved to Europe, taking Hecht's two young sons with her. His grief at their departure was 'paralyzing', and he was hospitalized for depression for three months, opting for treatment with drugs instead of the usual electro-shock. (Can you imagine what that might have erased from his brain?) He also went into psychotherapy, and that therapeutic introspection started to affect his poems—for the better, I'd say.

The Hard Hours opens with 'A Hill,' which announces the mature Hecht style and braces the reader for darker things to come. The poem begins with another Italian scene, but instead of elaborate stanzas about ejaculating fountains, we get unrhymed pentameter with narrative drive:

> In Italy, where this sort of thing can occur,
> I had a vision once—though you understand
> It was nothing at all like Dante's, or the visions of saints,
> And perhaps not a vision at all. I was with some friends,
> Picking my way through a warm sunlit piazza
> In the early morning. A clear fretwork of shadows
> From huge umbrellas littered the pavement and made
> A sort of lucent shallows in which was moored
> A small navy of carts.

The tone is conversational; the literary reference to Dante and the painterly description of the piazza are subordinate to the story. The carts belong to vendors in front of the Farnese Palace in Rome; the scene is full of color and noise.

> And then, when it happened, the noises suddenly stopped,
> And it got darker; pushcarts and people dissolved
> And even the great Farnese Palace itself
> Was gone, for all its marble; in its place
> Was a hill, mole-colored and bare. It was very cold,
> Close to freezing, with a promise of snow.
> The trees were like old ironwork gathered for scrap
> Outside a factory wall. There was no wind,
> And the only sound for a while was the little click
> Of ice as it broke in the mud under my feet.

The 'lucent shallows' have suddenly frozen, and we're in one of those bleak, desolate landscapes that express something fundamental about Hecht's inner being. We saw such a landscape in 'Christmas Is Coming', but from now on these scenes will feel intensely personal—and also universal. In 'A Hill', the vision is brief. The narrator finds himself back in the piazza, 'scared by the plain bitterness of what I had seen.' Years later, he remembers that he first saw the hill on a road 'north of Poughkeepsie; and as a boy / I stood before it for hours in wintertime.'

Hecht has said that some of the worst misreadings of his poems have been made by people who take them as strictly autobiographical, and I doubt that 'A Hill' is a literal recounting of a vision (though Hecht may be referring to a real hill—Bard College is in upstate New York, north of Poughkeepsie). But emotionally, the poem is absolutely true. As Hecht told Hoy, the reason a boy would stand for hours in such a place is that 'no one comes to take him away from all this barrenness.' Humanity at its bleakest is the underlying theme of *The Hard Hours*, and Hecht stands before it unblinkingly.

The toughest of its poems to read—and, I'm guessing, the toughest for Hecht to have written—is 'Rites and Ceremonies,' a long, searing meditation on the Holocaust that takes some of its form, and much of its feeling, from the liturgy of Yom Kippur, the Jewish holy day of fasting and repentance. The poem is woven from Biblical quotes, liturgical cadences and discourses on the persecution of Jews through history, all with a sonorous grave music. One section is called 'The Fire Sermon'—a title also used by Eliot in

'The Waste Land.' The Fire Sermon was Buddha's discourse on achieving liberation from suffering through detachment from the senses and mind, and in Eliot's poem, the detachment feels like neurotic disconnection. For Hecht, the detachment is a heroic attempt to lift himself out of the flames of the concentration camps and respond to what he has seen. Of course there is no possibility of a coherent response; yet the poem does cohere. It takes us inside the poet's mind and heart, capturing his individual despair and the despair of all of us that such things continue to happen on earth. 'The contemplation of horror is not edifying, / neither does it strengthen the soul', it says. But such contemplation is essential, and this poem proves it.

Another long poem in *The Hard Hours*, 'Three Prompters From the Wings', contemplates horror from a much greater distance. It's a retelling of the Oedipus legend from the viewpoints of the three Fates, and lofty as this may sound, it's quiet, wise and lyrical, a great pleasure to read. Hecht's choice of trimeter makes the tale unfold almost sweetly:

> But what, you ask, of the hero?
> …He advances without trembling
> From sorrow unto sorrow
> Toward a kind of light
> The sun makes upon metal
> Which perhaps even the blind
> May secretly behold.
> What the intelligence
> Works out in pure delight
> The body must learn in pain.
> He has solved the Sphinx's riddle
> In his own ligaments.

Two other important lyric poems referencing the Holocaust are collected here. One, '"More Light! More Light!"', compares the burning at the stake of a Renaissance Christian with the brutality of a guard at Buchenwald. The other, '"It Out-Herods Herod. Pray You, Avoid It"', has the poet contemplating his children's idea of good and evil in the light of what he knows about the world: '… in their fairy tales / The warty giant and witch / Get sealed in doorless jails / And the match-girl strikes it rich.' His children see their father as a mix of God and Santa Claus, but he knows better:

And that their sleep be sound
I say this Childermas
Who could not, at one time,
Have saved them from the gas.

Childermas is the feast commemorating Herod's slaughter of the innocents. I was born in the U.S. after 1950, with four Jewish grandparents who were American citizens, and these lines still represent the way I see the world.

The Hard Hours, justly, won major acclaim; fellowships, prizes, professorships and other honors followed in profusion from then on. Hecht's personal life was also happier. He married Helen D'Alessandro, a former student of his who became an interior designer and cookbook author, in 1971; the couple's son was born the following year.

I read the *Selected* from front to back, and by the time I got to Hecht's next two collections, *Millions of Strange Shadows* (1977) and *The Venetian Vespers* (1979), I could see he had become, if not exactly a ray of sunshine, more relaxed and expansive. In these poems—even the very serious ones—it's clear he's at the top of his game and having a wonderful time. He's still fond of complex stanzas peppered with deft allusions, but now there's greater wisdom and heart. In 'A Birthday Poem', written for his wife, he begins by describing a cloud of midges in the summer sun—something difficult for the eye to focus on, leaving the viewer 'unable certainly to say // What lies behind it, or what sets it off / With fine diminishings, / Like the pale towns Mantegna chose to place / Beyond the thieves and King of Kings…' This is a reference to a Renaissance painting of a crucifixion. Hecht loves to write about the impossibly tiny figures and landscapes in the backgrounds of such paintings, and here he meditates on the difficulty of seeing small things in the context of a larger whole:

It's the same with Time. Looked at *sub specie*
    Aeternitatis, from
The snow-line of some Ararat of years,
  Scholars remark those kingdoms come
To nothing, to grief, without the least display
Of anything so underbred as tears,

And with their Zeiss binoculars descry
    Verduns and Waterloos
The man-made mushroom's deadly overplus,

> Caesars and heretics and Jews
> Gone down in blood, without batting an eye,
> As if all history were deciduous.

Only by attending to the present moment is it possible to 'note / A curious excitement of the heart / And slight catch of the throat' that he feels in his wife's presence, or when he looks at a photograph of her as a child, on another birthday, in her new sneakers.

> The picture is black and white, mere light and shade.
>   Even the sneakers' red
> Has washed away in acids. A voice is spent,
>   Echoing down the ages in my head:
> *What is your substance, whereof are you made*
> *That millions of strange shadows on you tend?*

These are the first two lines of Shakespeare's Sonnet 53, in which the world's beauty and bounty are seen as shadows cast by the beloved. Birthdays fly by; we are as mutable as that cloud of midges; yet, amazingly, there is such a thing as a constant heart. The poem ends with Hecht's wonder and gratitude for his wife's love, which 'brims upon the world.' It is, in every possible way, a beautiful thing.

But it's the long narrative poems and dramatic monologues in unrhymed pentameter that most characterize the later collections. Normally I lack patience for such things. But I found I loved diving into these longer poems, reading them a second, a third, a fourth time, gaining greater understanding each time. Which is not to say I think I understand them completely. The narratives present a new kind of difficulty—not of densely packed literary allusion but of the shifting identity of the narrator. Hecht wants to reveal and disguise himself at the same time; his impulse is to 'Tell all the truth but tell it slant', as Emily Dickinson put it.

'Green: An Epistle', for example, begins with what must have been Hecht's boyhood experience of going to the movies at 'a giant Roxy, / Where the lights dimmed and the famous allegory / Of Good and Evil, clearly identified / …Seduced us straight into that perfect world / Of Justice under God.' But suddenly the narrator is 'safe / Here in this grubby little border town / With its one cheap hotel', writing a poem about the corruption of the soul in terms of the evolution of the plant world. (Okay, there is a literary reference here. The poem has an epigraph from one of Theodore

Roethke's greenhouse poems, in which the soul's struggle is compared to a cut plant straining to put down new roots.) Hecht told Hoy that the speaker in 'Green' is 'admittedly partly me', and that it's 'about the disguises of Pride', and about how suppressing the ego behind a façade of innocence leads to monstrous deformity of the spirit. Well, you could have fooled me. So much of the poem is taken up by gorgeous imagery of 'Rat-tailed, ambitious' flagellates evolving into 'Sequoia forests of vindictiveness' that one begins to wonder: Is this the sort of stuff Wallace Stevens would have written if he'd seen a therapist twice a week?

I had an easier time with 'Apprehensions', which is straightforwardly about Hecht's anxious, claustrophobic childhood in Depression-era New York. But it's also about learning to see, which, Hecht has said, is 'a crucially important act' of becoming. The boy looks out his apartment window as a storm comes up 'by dark gradations':

> The streets became more luminous, the world
> Glinted and shone with an uncanny freshness….
> The streetcar tracks gleamed like the paths of snails.
> And all of this made me superbly happy,
> But most of all a yellow Checker Cab
> Parked at the corner. Something in the light
> Was making this the yellowest thing on earth….
> It was the absolute, parental yellow.

The child's life is no happier after this, and the poem's ending foreshadows the horrors of the coming war. But the act of seeing is transformative.

The dramatic monologues in *The Venetian Vespers* are also full of pivotal acts of seeing, but in these poems, he hides behind other people's identities, not always successfully. The narrator of 'The Grapes' is a chambermaid at a Swiss mountain resort coming to the realization that she's past her prime. She sounds just like Anthony Hecht. The poem's central metaphor, though, is so compelling that you recognize her not as a specific fictional character but as a human being becoming conscious of the limits of her life. Her hotel is on the side of the mountain that's lit by sun in the morning and in shadow by late afternoon; it attracts 'a somewhat older, quieter clientele'. Across the valley is the Beau Rivage, whose younger 'patrons are laved / in generous tides of gold. At cocktail time / Their glasses glint like gems, while we're eclipsed.' One morning at breakfast, she sees her own eclipse in a sunlit bowl of green grapes in ice water.

Reflections of the water dodged and swam
In nervous incandescent filaments
Over my blouse and up along the ceiling.
And all those little bags of glassiness,
Those clustered planets, leaned their eastern cheeks
Into the sunlight, each one showing a soft
Meridian swelling where the thinning light
Mysteriously tapered into shadow…

That is one literary chambermaid. But she's telling me something important.

The main character in 'The Short End', an aging alcoholic named Shirley Carson, is also not convincing as a woman. We know where she's been, what she wore on her honeymoon and what sort of wreck her life has become, but she doesn't really have a voice of her own. Her world of kitsch and vulgarity sounds not-quite-right in Hecht's Olympian pentameter. It's no wonder that when he first showed this poem to friends, they would 'cough and avert their eyes, unable to tell me straight out that…I've gone into obvious literary decline' (from a letter to Joe Summers, a colleague at the University of Rochester).

If I had been schooled as a feminist critic, I might have stopped here. But once I got past this problem of voice, the poem became a kind of mid-century American 'Waste Land', a flight from spiritual pain into a fortress of cigarettes and alcohol. Shirley's America is a crude, barren place. She encounters a roadside attraction—a live entombment—that is an allegory of false resurrection, a church of hucksterism whose congregants are routinely lied to. She ultimately disappears into a *Drambuie* ad that becomes a vision of hell. The poem is actually quite an achievement.

Perhaps 'The Short End' feels forced because it was written in deliberate contrast to 'The Venetian Vespers', the magnificent long monologue whose troubled, neurotic narrator is partly based on an American expat Hecht once met in Italy. The poem accurately recounts the man's disturbing childhood, but it's the setting—'the grandeur and decay' of Venice, as Hecht called it—that truly expresses the narrator's state of soul. The poem contains pages and pages of stunning, disturbing description. It's one of Hecht's masterpieces; but the new Selected is full of masterpieces.

Hecht, like Brahms (that other master of classical form as a vehicle for deep emotion), was careful to publish only those works that were up to his very high standard. Also as with Brahms, the late works are as finely wrought as the earlier ones but sparer and more compressed. His natural melancholy acquires a soft, shimmering patina—there's no other way to describe it except in terms of light. The volume's last poem, "The Darkness and the Light are Both Alike to Thee", begins

> Like trailing silks, the light
> Hangs in the olive trees
> As the pale wine of day
> Drains to its very lees…

Day becomes night; lights appear in the plush darkness, and then those, too, fade with the approach of morning.

> Like the elderly and frail
> Who've lasted through the night,
> Cold brows and silent lips
> For whom the rising light
> Entails their own eclipse,
> Brightening as they fail.

This poet's eyes were open from beginning to end.

Kevin Hanson

Nietzsche and the Horse

It's not easy for a dispassionate person, Friedrich
Nietzsche discovered one day on the street, to find
the correct level of disdain for the Judeo-Christian
morality of the slave, its compassion for the herd,
when a horse is being whipped violently by a man.

For admirers of Nietzsche's morality of the master
and his will to power and the rest of his theoretical
justification for behaving badly, it was a blessing
when the Superman with his arms round the neck
of a suffering animal could be diagnosed insane.

Travis Mossotti

Delivering the Bad News

The waitress who wore varicose stockings
in Steffen's diner north of Yulee, Florida
rolled her eyes when I ordered a cup of coffee

in a manner suggesting that those in her tribe
often killed messengers sent to deliver bad news
or unwelcome travelers requesting hot drinks

and stretched men on the rack for far less than
a spilled glass of sweet tea, which was what everyone
down there, up there, depending, drank religiously,

till their yellowed teeth cramped up and drowned
and were replaced in a jiff by a set of $99 dentures
that would keep them gnawing the hind quarters

of torched animals for the millions of Friday nights
still to come, nights when the boys would slump
through the doors in defeat, in leg pads, would

sit down, probably in the booth I was sitting in,
and bury their heads into their hands to discover
the stark moment where youth grows pale.

Philip Rush

Mimo

As far as I'm concerned,
there's nothing to it,
and all that Narnia stuff
is seriously over-rated.

Down Sussex Gardens, for instance,
and with no sign of magic I can see,
you can open a wintry door
and enter Kosovo, watch Albanian television

and drink Balkan coffee
with a waitress who is as slender
as some sort of tree
unique to some particular Balkan slope.

She smiles exactly how
the sun came out over the Boleyn Ground.

Katrina Naomi

The Woman who Married the Berlin Wall

fell in love at the age of seven, thrilling
to this Berlinner's slim sensuality,
his horizontal lines, his sense of division;
found the Great Wall of China 'far too stout'.

She used the words 'he' or 'my husband',
made models of her lover, took him on sleigh rides
so he could enjoy her native northern Sweden.

She papered her rooms from bulging scrapbooks.
On her sixth visit, they wed: a small ceremony.
She scratched her desire deep into his core;
knowing he couldn't leave until he was demolished,
chunk by chunk. She felt she owned him outright.

I have some sympathy for a woman who could love a wall.
I have practised kissing tables, licking car seats,
have pressed myself against an aeroplane's wing.

Kona Macphee

Pheasant, Waverley Station

In diesel-stour so thick I'm loath
to bare my packaged sandwiches, he lies:
one red-ringed eye is signalling the sky,
the other pegs a sleeper. What long miles
he must have travelled in the undercarriage,
while flesh and mechanism reaffirmed
the compacts of their loveless marriage.

The Secret Life of Numbers

To goad the sting of a dozy hornet
and quantify its tot of agony;

to conjure the orbit of an exoplanet
from the pulse of a starry vagary;

to know in what measure the flowers, the sonnet
draw two bodies to their perigee;

to watch the uranium cloaked in granite
counting in half-lives, like an ovary.

Richard Wilbur on Creating *Candide*

Poet Richard Wilbur discusses working with Leonard Bernstein and Lillian Hellman on the creation of a classic American musical.

An Interview with Dana Gioia

GIOIA: *Dick, let's start at the very beginning. How did you become involved in writing the lyrics for Leonard Bernstein's* Candide?

WILBUR: Well, as my Uncle Stan always said on such occasions, it's a long story, but I love to tell it. I have to go back to about 1950. Lillian Hellman had done an excellent adaptation of Jean Anouilh's *The Lark*, and for it Lenny Bernstein had done five or ten minutes of incidental support-ing music. The play and the music had both succeeded very well with the public. In view of that success, it occurred to Lillian that she might adapt another clever Frenchman, and so she turned to Voltaire's *Candide*. For that project, too, she enlisted Bernstein to do some supplementary or incidental music. What happened is quite easy to imagine. Every time she wrote a beautiful scene based on Voltaire's *Candide*, Lenny would say, 'Lillian this is gorgeous, absolutely gorgeous; it's a great piece of playwriting; of course, it would make a very good musical number.' That happened over and over again until they found that what they had was developing into a musical show.

There had been some other potential lyricists in mind before you came along. What happened to them?

Well, once they found they had a developing musical show, they had to bring in some people to write the lyrics. The first person, though you won't believe this, was James Agee. I never saw any of Agee's lyrics for *Candide*, but I asked Hellman and Bernstein what they'd been like. They both said the same thing. They said they were too good. They were so good in a liter-ary way that they didn't require the supplemental support of music. So Mr. Agee left the show early, and in came Dorothy Parker. She worked with Bernstein on a couple of numbers and probably in the show's present state, there are still some lines written by Dorothy Parker. But she and Bernstein were not compatible, and she went home and wouldn't work on the show any more. So Hellman and Bernstein turned to a professional lyricist, John La Touche, who had a rather distinguished record, and who wrote, by the way, the two best lines that were ever written for *Candide*. Those lines went, 'What a day, what a day / For an *auto da fé.*' I can't give you a full account of his leaving the show. I don't know the reasons, but I believe they were personal. At the time I met Lillian Hellman at a party in Boston, around 1955, she and Bernstein were yet again in need of a lyricist.

It was a case of being in the right place at the right time.

Yes. I had some good advocates. Harry Levin, the noted Harvard professor of Comparative Literature, had said to Lillian Hellman that she might consider engaging me to write the lyrics because I had just done justice, so he felt, to another clever Frenchman—Moliére whose *Misanthrope* I had translated and which was then being performed in Cambridge and would be in New York the next year.

Had you ever written any song lyrics before Candide?

I think that an honest answer to that would be no. But back in my high school days, even in my younger days in college, I played the guitar and sang folk songs. All this, of course, was long before everyone else was doing it. I used to have 64 verses of 'Frankie and Albert,' for example, and I could sing you almost any other American folk songs or blues numbers. I did write the words for a few blues songs, but they were not deathless, and they did not prepare me to do the job for *Candide*.

Now I'm going to ask you the classic question everyone asks songwriters. What came first—the words or the music?

In this case, I was stepping into a show for which a certain amount of work had already been done. Sometimes because Lillian Hellman was frequently modifying the book, it was necessary to revise a number, and I did a certain amount of that by revising the lyrics of my predecessors. At other times Lillian would have produced a fine scene for us to pillage, and it would occur to me where a good song might be, and I would be allowed to write the lyric first. Then Lenny would see if he could set it. Sometimes Bernstein had already thought of the appropriate music for a situation that came up in Lillian's scenes. At other times I was a little quicker to think of something, and he agreed to set the words as they came.

So the answer is you did whatever worked.

That is exactly right.

What was it like to work with Leonard Bernstein? Reportedly, not everyone could do it.

Both Lenny and I wanted to be the whole cheese, of course, and we did quarrel, but we had a pretty good time on the whole. I was happy to work with someone who was so full of energy as he was and whose work I felt pretty sure was going to bear fruit. I felt I was on a winning team.

Lillian Hellman was also famously quarrelsome. What was your relationship like with Hellman, especially when you were 'pillaging' so many of her words?

Somehow she forgave me. We were very good friends then and always. But it was not lost on me (or on anybody) that it upset her to have her good scenes turned into musical numbers. So the whole experience of making *Candide* had a miserable side for her. But so far as I was concerned, she was a very good sport.

Did the writing of any song or scene give you particular trouble?

I think the most troublesome number was troublesome in prospect you might say. Lillian's book was faithful to the drift of Voltaire's novel, and both books end in ruefulness and lowered expectations. That's not what people want in a finale, you know. So as the finale approached, both Lenny and I kept hinting how can we be true to Voltaire? How can we end this story in a muted and rueful way and yet give the audience what they expect in the way of a finale? I hope that we found a good compromise. The words of the finale are very modest and rueful, and at the same time Lenny was able to take a line like 'And make our garden grow' and give it all the positiveness that the audience expects of a finale.

One of your songs was dropped from this first production. What song was it, and what did the producers find objectionable about the lyrics?

The producers, Ethel Reiner and Lester Osterman, were worried about the likely effect on certain New York reviewers of a number called 'Pangloss's

Song' or 'Dear Boy.' A number which is perhaps most closely based on Voltaire than anything else in our show. It comes at a point in the action where Candide, who has thought his master Pangloss dead, finds that he is alive but suffering from venereal disease. Candide asks him the question, 'Dear Dr. Pangloss, you told us that everything was for the best in this best of all possible worlds. How can this your lamentable physical condition be for the best?' Whereupon, Pangloss sings this song.

Would you be bold as to read the lyrics of this scandalous song?

I will be happy to do so, Dana. Here is Pangloss's song, 'Dear Boy':

> Dear boy, you will not hear me speak
> With sorrow or with rancor
> Of what has paled my rosy cheek
> And blasted it with canker;
> 'Twas Love, great Love, that did the deed
> Through Nature's gentle laws,
> And how should ill effects proceed
> From so divine a cause?
>
> Sweet honey comes from bees that sting,
> As you are well aware;
> To one adept in reasoning,
> Whatever pains disease may bring
> Are but the tangy seasoning
> To Love's delicious fare.
>
> Columbus and his men, they say,
> Conveyed the virus hither
> Whereby my features rot away
> And vital powers wither;
> Yet had they not traversed the seas
> And come infected back,
> Why, think of all the luxuries
> That modern life would lack!

> All bitter things conduce to sweet,
> As this example shows;
> Without the little spirochete
> We'd have no chocolate to eat,
> Nor would tobacco's fragrance greet
> The European nose.

I think that must be the finest rhyming of spirochete *in the English language.*

Yes, but I don't think it's rhymed a great deal. And our producers didn't like it being rhymed at all. But there it was, and Lenny had set it beautifully, and it was being sung very well. So I'm glad that it was shortly afterwards and forever reinstated in the show.

We are, too. Now Candide *was revised and restaged many times over the years with a variety of creative teams. What role did you play in these revisions?*

Lillian had said to Lenny that he could do anything he liked with the show after our initial experience at the Martin Beck Theater. I said pretty much the same thing. I gave him my permission to tinker with the show in any way that he felt would make it more successful. But at the same time I was always glad to help out with revisions and additional lyrics. I generally enjoyed doing so. I remember that when there was one version that we called the 'opera house' version, which was done, I expect, for the New York City Opera. I had the pleasure on that occasion of doing a fresh lyric in which I rhymed *selfish* and *shellfish*. You don't get the privilege very often.

Did you ever work on another musical?

Yes, I did. It was ultimately a sad story. About ten years after *Candide*, I was invited to write the lyrics for a musical version of *The Madwoman of Chaillot*, based on Jean Giraudoux's delightful play. Maurice Valency had done an original book and Michel Legrand was going to be the composer. I signed on, glad to do it, because it was going to be a quality project. We wrote many excellent songs for the *Madwoman*, and we had reached the point of casting—asking people to sing a few of the songs so that we could judge their potentialities. The producer, who shall be nameless, an idiotic amateur, lost control of the adaptation rights, and therefore we could not proceed with the show. *The Madwoman* fell into the hands of Jerry Herman who produced a show called *Dear World*.

Do you have any other favorite memories of working on Candide?

There are several happy memories. I remember that when we were in Boston doing our out of town tryouts, all of us, Tyrone Guthrie, Lillian, Lenny, and I, used to meet, for heaven's sake, in the lounge of the Men's Room of the Wilbur Theater. (It was a better place than it sounds.) We had a long table and six chairs. At one of our deliberations it was agreed that somehow toward the end of the final act during the scenes in Venice something went a little dumb or numb, something ceased to delight the audience. We thought it might lie in the book, but no, that didn't seem to be the guilty party. We even thought it might have to do with the colors of the scenery, but at last we were forced to admit that what was needed was a new number. Although I'm not always brilliant about thinking of new numbers, I did so on that occasion. I outlined the possibility of the number called 'What's The Use?' in which four gamblers would express their different catastrophic experiences. Everybody said please go execute it. So I went back to my hotel room and began writing the lyrics. As they came, I carried them over to Leonard Bernstein's hotel room, and he began immediately setting them to music. We had a complete number by midnight. Hershy Kay was awakened to orchestrate it, and we were able to put it into rehearsal the next afternoon. One day later it was in the show, and it considerably pepped up that moment we'd been worrying about.

In your experience, how is writing a song lyric different from writing a poem or similar to writing a poem?

Well, they're really very different. I remember somebody pointing out to me that given the right music and the right situation, 'I love you' is a brilliant line. That can't be said on the whole about poetry. A song lyric needs to be very simple in its vocabulary, so that the tired man from Scarsdale in the fifth row doesn't miss the point of it in the first line. The lyrics need to be easy to pronounce, and they need to be repetitive, making their point again and again in a pleasing way. They need to be emotionally simple. A poem can be much different from that, of course. It can be more difficult. It can be much more ambiguous and subtle than one can manage to be in a show lyric. That's a beginning of an answer.

You have now translated every major comedy by Molière except Dom Garcie de Navarre, *which, as you have pointed out, was a dud. Did translating Molière influence your work on* Candide? *And did working on Broadway influence your subsequent versions of Molière's comedies?*

I think there isn't too much connection between the two kinds of work. In one case I'm translating faithfully. In the other case I'm abetting a transformation into a play. The main thing I carried over from translating Molière was a feeling for elegance. I wanted to find what kind of comparable elegance might belong to Voltaire. And do justice to him.

One final question. Thomas Hardy prefaced his book Winter Words *with a boast that no other poet (at least no major poet) had ever published a book in his 89th year. At the age of 89, which is to say in your 90th year, you have just published a fine new book of poems. It doesn't appear that you believe in retirement. Would you be willing to read us a poem from your new book,* Anterooms?

I certainly will, though I'm only beating Mr. Hardy by 12 months. Here's a poem which comes of the fact that although I was born in New York City, I've become a hick. And every now and then I write something defiant toward the city and the suburbs. The poem is called 'Out Here':

> Strangers might wonder why
> That big snow-shovel's leaning
> Against the house in July.
> Has it some cryptic meaning?
>
> It means at least to say
> That, here, we needn't be neat
> About putting things away,
> As on some suburban street.
>
> What's more, by leaning there
> The shovel seems to express,
> With its rough and ready air,
> A boast of ruggedness.

If a stranger said in sport
'I see you're prepared for snow,'
Our shovel might retort
'Out here, you never know.'

Thank you, Richard Wilbur.

Angela Leighton

Fen Elegy

It leaves no house-room for the unhouselled waif,
no shift for the shiftless, livings for the late—
the sun's broad sweep is gold on a plate.

It lets no hideaway, suffers no shade
for the holy wanderer, fetch in a wood-glade.
The levels extend their feathery brocade

of wood-rush, fen-sedge, reed-mace, lines
to fringe a world's edge, filter the big skies.
It's an open hand of riverring lifelines.

So cut the reed-beds, strip the willow,
channel the washes, level the hollow—
for the lilywhite boys will be gone tomorrow.

A. B. Jackson

Easter Monday

Morningkind, we sail our Easter bed.
Moves get sprung: an Octopus, a Lovelock,
some wrestlemania before we mate,

biting our soft coin, exchanging gifts.
Shoulders pinned, I offer my sea-chains,
a billy goat also, to minister these rocks,

and fifty-seven varieties of shame.
You stroke my fur, give me your best licks,
a miracle fish made of cellophane.

Weedy otters amaze with brave high-jinx
but we're agog as bodies dewdrop, glisten,
quicken towards O, this mounting crisis.

We lie lapwinged as dawn rises.
Long live critters in caves, in earth, in ashes.

An Enquiry Concerning Mouse Brightness

A shoebox burial in summer soil:
the mouse Mickey, pet, formerly pink
eyed, gone stiff, plain gone, Platonic,

the pure idea of Mouse, not monster mouse
or twitch augmented, no diminished
fifth or seventh or jazz funeral James

Bond style, no: a circa '73 garden willow,
shallow hole, that shoebox, a mouse
in exile, in excelsis, poor Crusoe.

The vigil was night-long, with snacks—
arise, arise you teardrop flame of blue,
you Esso blue, you gas-pilot: a soul

unhoused, un-moused, most visible, oh
and beaming up, to Enterprise, amen.

Helena Nelson

Blackadder, Polypton and Fruitcake

> Who is it that says most? which can say more
> Than this rich praise, that you alone are you?
> —Sonnet 84

I began reading this book on a train travelling between Glasgow and Edinburgh. I had to change at Haymarket to get back to Fife, so I continued my task in the chilly little waiting room on platform 4. I was deeply absorbed and missed two trains. When re-reading the book some months later, on a train from Haymarket to Markinch, I very nearly missed my stop, scrambled off the train in some disarray and left my favourite scarf behind (but not the book). It was not entirely Don Paterson's fault. William Shakespeare had something to do with it.

I have been digesting bits of Shakespeare, on and off, all my life, or so it seems. I re-read at least one of the plays carefully each year. I go back to the Sonnets about every ten years, when a new edition catches my eye, or a friend is reading them and I'm drawn in. I am no sonnet superhero. I don't have them all by heart, but I have learned half a dozen or so at different times, and I can *almost* remember those few. They taught me all I know, if indeed I know it, about the way sound and sense in poetry can be one and the same.

The danger of reading a new commentary on poems you love, of course, is that the writer has entered personal territory. A reading that conflicts with your own is an emotional event, not just a matter of polite interest. And these are *Shakespeare*'s Sonnets. A permanent hubbub of attention surrounds them. When you read them quietly on your own, you possess them. You forget the other people with emotional and intellectual investment in this hot property. But then a book like this reminds you, and there's a little shiver of excitement.

It's not just the Sonnets that generate continuous commentary; the commentaries themselves generate fevered response. Who is it that says most? The Paterson book was reviewed in all the major UK newspapers, in several leading blogs and even four times (so far) on Amazon. Behold the star-studded cast: Hugh Thomson (*The Independent*), Adam Mars-Jones (*The Observer*), Christopher Rush (*The Herald*), Robert McCrum (*The Guardian*), Jonathan

Reading Shakespeare's Sonnets: A New Commentary by Don Paterson. Faber and Faber, 2010.
ISBN 978 0 571 24502 4; 500 pp; £17.99, hbk.

Bate (*The Financial Times*), Daniel Swift (*The Spectator*), Adam O'Riordan (*The Telegraph*), Alastair Fowler (*The Times Literary Supplement*) and the inimitable Peggy Hughes (*The Scotsman*). If it was reviewed in *The Irish Times*, I couldn't find it—but there may be specific reasons why not (more of that later). The observant reader will note the unusual gender of the last reviewer on my list. The only other female comments I have found on the Paterson book (so far) are the blogger 'DoveGreyReader' and Amazon reviewer Mrs Jane Hawkes, 'Livefats', (Lancashire). It seems plain that when an author sends out a challenge to members of the academic fraternity who, like me, 'own' the Sonnets, it takes a Man to deal with the upstart.

Don Paterson, in this volume, doesn't pretend to write as a scholar. This is a book by a jobbing poet, a university teacher and 'big trope-hunter'. It is, he says, 'a reading diary' written 'quite intentionally, in a tearing hurry. . . .' Writing and reading in spare pockets of time was, he explains, a way of contending with the question: 'What are these poems to *me* now?' The resulting volume is personal ('Poetry *demands* of us a personal response'), unlike scholarly criticism which is 'necessarily impersonal in nature' and must, by implication, resist that demand. Perhaps.

As some readers will already know, the prefatory comments about Paterson's aims did not protect him from pre-emptive strikes. Most reviewers praised his lively approach to the task, but there were noteworthy exceptions. Adam Mars-Jones remarked on the book's unevenness (equivalent only to the Sonnets themselves). He disliked the tone, the way it mixed 'academic discourse, often lively' with 'internet chatroom rambling'. He remarked on the difference between the style of this book and 'the fastidiousness' of the author's own poetry. He made the point (validly, I think) that Paterson was not in a good position to comment on the way Sonnet 144 unnecessarily shared distasteful opinions, given some of the opinions he himself jocularly aired, not least the fact that 'it's quite impossible . . . not to be reminded of the current 'plight' of the Catholic church. Don't get me wrong—I'm sure many priests signed up because they were career paedophiles and saw a splendid opportunity.' Yes—perhaps *not* going to be a candidate for review in *The Irish Times*.

Robert McCrum found 'his candour . . . thrilling.' However, while 'Some Bardophiles will love it,' he observed sagely, 'Others will not.' Quite. However, McCrum hadn't finished reading it when he wrote these comments, which meant he hadn't even got as far as the career paedophiles. By far the most serious onslaught was from Alastair Fowler in *The Times Literary Supplement*. Fowler is both an academic and a poet, of course, and he writes well. He is restrained, well-informed and precise—apparently. At first, it appeared to be Paterson's style that rubbed him up the wrong way. But once under full steam, he attacked DP's claim to an 'original' theory about the identity of the 'Rival Poet' and apparently made mincemeat of it, not to mention DP's suggestion that Kit Marlowe was 'the familiar ghost' in Sonnet 86: '. . . the identification of Marlowe as the familiar ghost was made by Thomson, Dover Wilson and Clare Campbell in her independent commentary (1979, 1999 and 2009).' Match point Fowler.

But wait. The following week, Paterson struck back. In the letters column of the *TLS*, there was a forceful rebuttal: 'I did not claim one ounce of originality for the theory that Chapman is the Rival Poet in Sonnet 86' (I must have misread this too, because I took the phrase 'entirely original' to mean no less). But DP goes on:

> The Marlowe as 'affable familiar ghost' theory was certainly news to a number of Shakespeare scholars of my acquaintance; but contrary to Fowler's assertion, J. Dover Wilson identifies Homer, not Marlowe, as the affable familiar ('This I believe is another allusion to . . . a false Homer'); J. A. K. Thomson also thinks it 'Homer's anima, who came to visit him [Chapman] from Elysium'. As for Clare Campbell's 'independent commentary', I can find no record of it anywhere. Perhaps Fowler meant to type 'S. C. Campbell', author of *Shakespeare's Sonnets Edited as a Continuous Sequence*, published by Cassandra Press—whose very occasional output, as far as I can ascertain, appears largely to consist of books by a single author—with which I am as familiar as I suspect he is.

Few things are as enjoyable and intriguing as a literary spat observed from the sidelines. Who was Clare Campbell, whose several independent commentaries spanned, according to Fowler's citations, no fewer than 40 years? Paterson suggests the seasoned *TLS* critic is 'happy to misrepresent for his own ends'. So did Fowler make it all up? The good Professor has remained silent. However, he did go on to dismember Stephen Greenblatt's *Will in the World: How Shakespeare became Shakespeare* in the same publication approximately a fortnight later.

The story's not quite over. On February 11th, the mysterious Clare Campbell appeared in the *TLS* letters column in person. This time there was no rattling of great antlers, as in the Paterson / Fowler contretemps. She pointed out quietly (and briefly) that her first book was neither self-published (presumably the rest of her books were), nor ignored: it was reviewed by no other than Katherine Duncan-Jones in the *TLS*, May 9, 1980. She corrects Paterson on the 'originality' dispute, too. It was not, apparently, the theory that Chapman was the rival poet in Sonnet 86 that Fowler took issue with. It was the theory that Marlowe was the ghost who helped Chapman—and Campbell claims this as *her* original suggestion. By which time, the ordinary reader no longer cares.

Which means Paterson is home and dry, with his only serious critic beaten at his own game. And now I find myself in a difficult position, because I loved Paterson's book. It gave me profound satisfaction for a whole variety of reasons, which I haven't even begun to rehearse yet. But I don't want him to get off scot-free. Fowler evidently dislikes him, for reasons that may remain as obscure to us as aspects of the Sonnets. We certainly don't need to know them. But before I go into a paean of praise and start quoting all my favourite bits, as other reviewers have joyfully done, let me consider some of the points raised by Fowler to which DP did not (really) reply.

If you examine Fowler closely, it would appear that his irritation with DP's style has prevented him reading accurately. This in itself suggests that DP has succeeded in one of his primary aims: 'to come up with something that was at least as annoying, [as Helen Vendler] even if it's only a tenth as smart'. (The comment about smartness is disingenuous: Paterson is one smart cookie.) He is having his copy of Vendler's *The Art of Shakespeare's Sonnets* 'rubberized', he tells us, 'so [he] can catch it again after [he's] thrown it at the wall'. I imagine Fowler hurled DP's book at the wall too, but without the rubber. And that he read it fast, spitting as he turned the pages, and hunting for errors.

But that's okay: I hunted for errors too, and found lots. In my case, they were proof-reading errors, but that didn't prevent my enjoyment. Paterson's book is, among countless other things, funny. I chortled all over the place, as well as nodded, tutted, shook my head and howled with laughter. Humour is one of the things you simply can't predict: what one person loves, another loathes. And there were comical parts I *didn't* find funny—for example, sonnet 152 ('In loving me thou know'st I am forsworn') rendered in 'EastEnders-speak', which doesn't work at all, so far as I can see, whereas 112 ('Your love and pity doth th'impression fill') taken apart surgically ('OK. Suit up, scrub up, and on with the gloves') gets my vote.

Even the *East Enders* bit—well, I think Paterson starts to run out of steam a little bit, especially towards the end, and also slightly in the middle. He took on a gargantuan task doing this book, not least because he was attempting to keep one eye on a whole set of other commentaries. He must have enormous energy, but even so . . . .

Back to Fowler, though. He suggests Paterson 'adopted the idiom of his audience' in the manner of 'many charismatic lecturers'. Down with charisma! The book is not written in 'Paterson's own style' but that 'of an imagined tutor struggling over the generation gap, fatally yielding to the temptation to be one of the boys. . . .' Myself, I think the style *is* Paterson's own. This is him, talking. He dips and swerves naturally from 'the ground is pulling itself apart in semantic antithesis' to 'the old "penis as bludgeon" trope hasn't done it for me in a long while.' And you either go with him willingly—participate in a conversation in which he exposes a great deal of himself—or you reject, as Fowler has done. Most readers will willingly enter Paterson's interaction, I suspect, even if it alienates them in places.

Paterson is not, as Fowler suggests, guilty of 'prejudice against poetic diction'—that's a misreading. The truth is rather the reverse, which might annoy some readers much more. DP's criticisms of Shakespeare are made in the context of 'love, for better or worse'; his 'I'd still take the least of WS's poems over just about anyone else's best' is anything but 'perfunctory'.

The deciding factor, in Paterson's assessment of each sonnet, is not, as Fowler suggests, 'transparency' and it is deliberate distortion to suggest that he 'likes poems he can understand right away' (and by inference, *dis*likes 'difficult' texts). 'As a poet,' says Fowler, 'Paterson knows how poetry should be read.' Sarcasm, in this instance, is a low form of wit. Paterson is much funnier, and when *he* is sarcastic, it's often so dead-pan you might not notice: 'For me, the most effective English sonnets employ a kind of double volta, and graft to the Italian a second turn at the couplet, taking advantage of the national talent for the parting shot.'

Fowler doesn't like Paterson's paraphrases, especially the burlesques (I do) and he finds what he calls the 'digressions' mainly padding (I found them, in turn, hilarious, fascinating, relevant, educative, provocative, infuriating and riveting, but never—not even during a mini-essay on transferred epithet—boring).

Fowler ends with his biggest gripes: first Paterson's need 'to rubbish the work of those who have helped him most'. (DP's epistolary riposte rightly rejected that). Secondly, he mentions a need 'to show the superiority of modern poetry to "that Shakespearian Rag"'. (I thought he did precisely the reverse.) Fowler ends with a series of questions, one of which scores a point: 'Why did he not correct his proofs?'

Of course, DP *did* correct his proofs. However, something must have gone wrong because the edition in my hands contains errors, omissions and confusions (in one case 'erotic' instead of 'acrostic') that I think must be unintentional and should have been picked up by a copy-editor, if not the author—even the Sonnets themselves are not fault-free. I imagine this book will sell extremely well so there will be an opportunity to correct a second edition. But it needs rigorous scrutiny.

And what about the instruction on 'how to read' the Sonnets? Paterson sets out his approach clearly in his introduction and it is interesting for all sorts of reasons, not least because it challenges the way we often engage with poetry today, looking for 'deep' meanings before we enjoy the text on its simplest level. Many contemporary readers, he suggests, 'assume that the poem is something that has to be translated before it can be meaningful, and that 'meaning' is something the poet has deliberately withheld. It doesn't and they didn't.'

That's the beginning of a thread that runs right through the volume, because one of the things Paterson weaves into his commentary is a set of observations about both poetic practice and reading 'rules'. For me, this was a particular attraction, but I'm biased since I largely share his views. Not everyone will. However, Paterson thrives on provocation. I don't think he cares whether or not you agree with him. It's natural to him to write persuasively and to argue his corner with what is often (all too lightly, these days) termed 'passion', because he feels absolutely sure he's right. Fair enough. Besides, as he says himself, 'Folk don't always realise how much sheer brass neck this job [poetry] takes.'

So he goes for a 'primary reading' that 'engages with the poem directly, as a piece of trustworthy human discourse'. This, he suggests, yields three things: 'what the poem is saying; what the poem is saying about us; and what the poem is saying about the author.' If we are 'to claim [the Sonnets] as great poems now, we have to show them as poems still capable of inviting and rewarding [this] kind of primary reading . . . and this is what this book sets out to do.'

And succeeds, I think. The reading we're invited to share is Paterson's own, and his skill for communicating a personal response is beyond doubt. Take a look at him starting on Sonnet 88 ('When thou shalt be dispos'd to set me light'):

> This looks like nothing, and indeed it isn't much; but the argument reveals the speaker as mentally unbalanced, if you ask me. It's *utterly* bizarre.

And 61 ('Is it thy will, thy image should keep open / My heavy eyelids to the weary night?'):

> It's clear that he's thinking, 'I know, I know. All the jealousy's on my side. OK, I'm just going to lie here, sweating in the dark, imagining the worst for the next four hours. Hey, it's a hobby.'
> The *agony* in this poem!

Paterson doesn't suggest he's articulating the only possible response, and that's just as well, because in a number of cases, my reaction to poems was significantly different from his—and that in itself was fun. I found myself jumping up and down and 'Yes but . . . ing' as if I had him there. I will never discuss any of these sonnets again without adducing this volume as at least one voice in the altercation. Furthermore, the whole approach to 'primary reading' is liberating: 'Reading a Shakespeare sonnet is an act of authorship,' says DP. 'Some of the time this will involve violently disagreeing with the reading of *this* reader.'

But this is not all he has to say about 'how to read'. There are a number of passages on how to read aloud (the practicalities of enunciation, pitch and emphasis); how to read critically ('Sensible criticism should surely consist in discovering a poem's own ambitions, and measuring its success or failing against *them*, not those of the poem you'd prefer to be reading'); how and why to read for primary sense ('always take the shortest route to literal sense, otherwise there's a good chance you'll just make something up'); how and why we should also 'read the author'; and finally how to go about reading this particular sequence of sonnets: 'The Sonnets have to be read as a narrative of the progress of love.'

Oddly, it's the last of these that causes me difficulty. Paterson's book hinges on the idea of tracking a love affair (with not only the Young Man—or men—and the Dark Lady, but also, I think, with love itself and poetry itself) from the initial stage of falling in love, through infatuation, constancy, jealousy, despair and (in the final sequence) misogynistic bitterness.

I've never read the Sonnets as a novel before, tracking the love 'plot' in all its emotional convolutions, although, like everyone else, I've always been aware of the love triangle surfacing at various points. Neither do I have any difficulty with Paterson's allegation that these are 'screamingly autobiographical poems'—the particular rawness of some of them seems to me to indicate this beyond doubt. Paterson works from the premise that the running order was chosen by Shakespeare himself; the love narrative is therefore deliberately developed. I *liked* reading the Sonnets this way, from beginning to end, with DP as story guide. But I wasn't persuaded this was the only way to go.

In the early poems, with their baffling emphasis on getting one poor young man to breed, I love the way Paterson's analysis shows how the personal tone gradually creeps into what are probably commissioned poems. I relish the way he develops this later, too, even to the point where he shows the connection between the inevitable end of the sequence looming and the parallel cooling of passion. It's when I reach the final set, the Dark Lady sonnets, that I'm uneasy with the reading, albeit beautifully articulated, that 'with the YM he was in the grip of a pure love, but stalked by the presence of lust: with the DL he is in the grip of a pure lust, but stalked by the absence of love.'

Paterson sees the author of the Sonnets as clearly homosexual, rather than bisexual, with a disturbing dislike of women, revealed unpleasantly in some of the poems. I'm not convinced by this, nor his readiness to sum up Shakespeare as a 'gay' man, as though that contemporary adjective clarifies anything. One's gender and sexual orientation *do* affect one's reading, I think, like it or lump it, but I would have thought a heterosexual woman (yep, that's me) would be more, not less, likely to find the sequence from 127 to 152 misogynistic. It has never struck me this way: it's always seemed to me that Shakespeare was in love with the mistress whose 'eyes are nothing like the sun', just as he was in love with the fair young man. The central emotion in that last set of sonnets seems to me to be sexual jealousy, that primitive passion which has such strange effects on human behaviour and thinking, now as then. 'The Dark Lady sonnets', says Paterson, 'are remarkable testament to how little an intelligent man can know about himself'. Or a remarkable testament to confusion, frustration, jealousy, betrayal and despair. Perhaps it's the same thing.

It did occur to me that in the act of writing the book, the engagement with 154 intense little poems predisposed a certain way of reading the last few, and that exhaustion alone can serve to highlight negative reading. I have never felt, while reading these poems, that Shakespeare hated women. However, it is perfectly clear that he hates *this* woman at the point of writing: he feels gulled and betrayed by her, and by the YM. Hell—they're both younger than him. He's in a vile situation, and morally compromised, of course. He chooses to blame her more. *Is* this misogyny? Would we not all blame one person for tempting the other? And doesn't it seem *worse* to be let down by a woman—the innocent repository of unreasonable expectations (see Hamlet's disillusionment with his mother and girlfriend, and Othello's unbalanced attraction to the idea of Desdemona's harlotry). Is it not quite logical that one reaction to this should be disgust with sex?

One of Paterson's stated intentions is to explore the degree to which these poems still speak to us, still have a 'useful' application. Sexual jealousy is as alarming and dangerous as it ever was, and the unreasonable disgust that comes through some of the final poems could not be more relevant to a contemporary reader. One thing the poet demonstrates all too clearly is the danger of thinking a person wonderful—the risk of love, effectively. One slip on their part and before we know it we're thinking *not* that the person is a little less goddess-like (or god-like) than we anticipated, but that they're evil past redemption. It all gets dirty.

Don Paterson gleefully takes time out from the troubling business of bad taste and misogyny by comical 'versions' of 135 and 136, the two I think of as 'the willy sonnets'. This is hilarious, but I think part of the driving force is that Paterson is getting tired, and laughing at Shakespeare is like getting the giggles in Church. I am unable to read this bit of his 'translation' without laughing:

> *Wilt thou, whose will is large and spacious,*

> —Won't you, whose desire is large and fanny is as capacious as a
>   wizard's sleeve

> *Not once vouchsafe to hide my will in thine?—*

> —allow me to play 'hide the salami' just the once?

There's more, much more. It is as good as the best bits of Blackadder, and also fascinating to watch how DP combines horseplay with asides like '*gracious* rhymes with *spacious*—they'd normally be disyllabic but here they're trisyllabic—*gray-she-us, spay-she-us.* SB thinks they're disyllabic but he's wrong: WS never drops a syllable in a strong-stress position . . .').

But this is a rich fruit-cake of a commentary. It's not just about Shakespeare. Paterson is doing many different things at once, and again, I think he can't help it. It's how his brain works (he alone is him). For example, there's ongoing interaction with other commentators, whom DP calls the 'dramatis personae' of the reading. This is often part of the entertainment, but also has the effect of inviting you to the party. I dug out my other Sonnets volumes, and also acquired Katherine Duncan-Jones and Helen Vendler because it's really fun—seeing what they all say—and then working out how you feel yourself. You could spend a year of your life doing nothing else, and at the end you would be enriched. You don't have to be a scholar—and that's a way in which this book is truly generous. It reminds you that what we have here is our common heritage. We really do, each of us, own these poems.

Then there's the barrage of 'interesting facts' that pop up periodically. Things like the fact that the Elizabethans didn't have the possessive 'its'; that Dowson was the first person to use the word 'soccer' in English. Some of the 'facts' are even fabricated on the spot—the 'universal law' that two poets can't share a muse, for example, or that fact that two writers overheard in conversation will have 'a 50 per cent chance' of talking about money.

There are two little essays at the end—one on the sonnet form and one on metre—but there are other essay-type diversions throughout the book, particularly on metaphor in various shapes and forms, analysis of argument, form and poetic technique from the point of view of the jobbing poet. At times this gets pretty deep, and DP often sounds the 'anorak alert' sirens, especially when he starts on Greek terms, which I started to list as I went through: *aposiopesis, hypallage, hyperbaton, antimeria, polyptoton, epizeuxis, epiphonema, antanaclasis, hendiadys,* to name but a few. I have difficulty with some of these because the derivations don't make immediate sense to me and I'm sadly literal at times. Even explanations of metaphor in terms of 'vehicle' and 'tenor', though perfectly reasonable, don't prevent me visualising Pavarotti driving a Cinquecento. And the more a person talks about metaphor, the more one becomes conscious of the way they're using more metaphors to explain what the first metaphor is doing, and that has a funny effect on me, like looking into multiple mirrors. But it's never less than fascinating.

It's clear that Paterson anticipates some of his readers will be poets because he discusses tricks of the trade at various points, and doles out barbed advice: '. . . overpublication is a terrible thing in a poet, and only arouses suspicion'. But then he also anticipates non-poet readers, because there are warnings too 'to all those thinking about embarking on an affair with a poet: all those sonnets aren't really about *you*, you know.' Above all there's a growing sense, as you work your way through, that whatever kind of reader you are, you're a trusted buddy. You are in private conversation with DP. It's even in the annotations ('*humour*: temperament. You knew that.'). It is endearing.

And there is insight. Some of the poems are discussed most beautifully. In Sonnet 134 ('So now I have confessed that he is thine') he combines his trope-hunter skills wonderfully with analysis of feeling. In Sonnet 60, ('Like

as the waves make towards the pebbled shore'), his own sense of the relationship between form and meaning is more persuasive than Jancis Robinson
on a great Bordeaux:

> The very lines of this poem feel like they're beating away at
> the great void on the right-hand side of the page, where all
> the white silence lives—driving against it, receding, driving
> against it again, enacting their own determined but doomed
> stay against it.

In his discussion of Sonnet 82 ('I grant thou wert not married to my
Muse'), his commentary helped me understand something about the source
of power in these poems I've never understood before. It's too long for me
to quote here (read the book) but it's a piece of remarkable, inspirational
writing about Shakespeare.

So—unless the quirky, disreputable, irrepressible style is an alienating
factor (I think it's what drove Fowler to distraction)—*Reading Shakespeare's
Sonnets* will make you want to read the Sonnets, and then to read them again,
and again. Which can say more than this rich praise?

Richie McCaffery

The Rapture

Yesterday was Judgment Day.
We were stuck on an inter-city bus
in a traffic jam like a fleet of clippers
threaded through the neck of a cod's bottle,
an exodus on a single lane road.

Somewhere in God's granite allotment plots,
nanotechnologies of hatred and grudges
were stirring the blessed restful soil,
the dead limbering up for a carious dash
to the hot seat, stray dogs salivating.

Cars dropped in ditches like windowsill flies,
a petrol tanker was the first to run out of fuel.
The wind turned punk, we were stuck for hours,
a man began to cry, a busload bound for eternity
unable to stand each other for a sweaty evening.

Only those with a destination will be lost.
You woke and spoke of maybe next year
for your firstborn, coming off the pills for good.
My watch hit six and the light was snatched away
as raindrops danced like sperm on the window.

Claire Askew

Dream Lover

He'd be in his own league, not like other men:
he'd have a big throbbing bike and bad tattoos—a heart
that said Mom, a flaming skull, pin-up in a see-through dress.
He'd know how to hot-wire a Ferrari in the dark,
eyes closed. He'd smell like kerosene and a quiet road at night,
and touch my face as if I'd made him blind.

Come on. We all know love isn't really blind.
This boy would have looks like a loaded gun, a menace
loose in leather pants. The hunk. Big stud. Not-so-white knight.
The face that dodged a thousand jealous fists. The King of Hearts.
He'd sleep all day and come out only after dark:
a smooth-tongued, new-age Dracula, and similarly dressed.

Gentleman of the road, he'd have no fixed address
but live in suites in cheap hotels: mini-bars and slatted blinds
and creaking beds. The kind of place you don't go after dark.
He'd ply me with drink and ask about my other men.
I'd say that they were slow and quiet of heart
compared to him. Unsure, polite: the stuff of nightmares.

I'd sneak out in shades and visit him nightly,
infatuated—a tattoo healing under my dress,
the mark of him. He'd spurn me in public, sicken my heart,
but later grind me down to the bones, swear blind
that this was love. He'd take the tired lines of previous men
and hypnotise me with them, like fireflies in the dark.

He'd have one brown eye and one blue—half darkness,
half cold flame—a blowtorch waiting to ignite.
He'd charm my mother, pay my tab and mend
my car; harass the boss on my behalf, address
my landlord strife with just a look. It's not that I'd be blind
to all his flaws—he'd have none, save his black, fictitious heart.

And of course I'd love his blackened heart
the most—this man who comes to find me in the dark.
We meet in tangled dreams that shift the blinds,
kick off the sheets, repeat—exquisite nightmare
I can never own. No relics left on the bedside dresser,
no hurried note—a phantom, unreal, never meant.

His name on my arm inside a heart, I rise,
dress blindly in the sucking dark, stalk out. My plan:
to search the town, the night for such a man.

Niall Campbell

The Fraud

How like a shepherd or herdsman of loss
I must have whistled out into the evening,
that a childhood dog came cowering to my heel;
years under, its coat now wool-thick with soil
and loosely collared with the roots of bog-myrtle.

A surprise then my old companion strained
to sneak by me to the fire and my wife.
Checked by a boot, it bore, not a dog's teeth,
but a long, black mouth, then slunk back to the hill.
At night I hear the thin dog claw our door.

Alasdair Macrae

The Law and Some Grace: Iain Crichton Smith

W E CAN TRACE THROUGH REFERENCES IN HER LETTERS something of
the gestation of Elizabeth Bishop's wonderful poem 'The Moose'.
There was a moment of conception in 1946 but the delivery did not take
place until 1972 when Bishop had a turmoiled labour to get it out. She had
thought in 1956 that it was due and announced so to her aunt but the process
was to take much longer. Iain Crichton Smith (with his Free Church back-
ground) was no Bishop. His productivity was extraordinary in speed, variety and volume. Novels, essays, plays, short stories as well as poems poured
from him for forty-five years in Gaelic and English. His collected short stories, in English, amount to twelve hundred pages. Nonetheless, some poems
continued to be rewritten or revisited, as if he was issuing progress reports
on his changing attitudes and emotional responses. In a late poem, 'Old
Woman', published posthumously, he writes: 'I see the old woman behind
the flowering broom. / I have followed her from poem to poem' and in
another, entitled 'The Old Woman', in the same collection *A Country for
Old Men*, he admits:

> It took me a while to push her down,
> the old woman dressed in black, into the graveyard
> and listen to the music of the wind.
>
> And learn to love the ripe corn and stubble
> and the voice of the young man who sang all day
> and the horizon which cut the sky like a knife.

In the Index to the *New Collected Poems* there are twenty-two titles which
include the word 'old', and, in most of these poems, the 'old' collocates with
'woman'. Whatever the other psychological elements in his development
(he was only one when his father died and he was a sickly child guarded and
dominated by his mother who lived with him until her death in 1972), the
figure of an older woman, stoical, strictly religious, implacable and unaffec-
tionate, was a demanding presence in his poetry until he was in his fifties.

It is excellent that so much of his poetry is made re-available, particularly for a new generation of readers. In the thirteen years since his death,

New Collected Poems by Iain Crichton Smith, edited with an introduction by Matthew McGuire. Carcanet, 2011. 546pp. £18.95 ppk.

references to his work have become scarcer but this is a fate which has been visited on many of his older colleagues in the craft. That amazing generation of Scottish poets centred on but challenging, defying, and extending from the great MacDiarmid, has recently suffered neglect or sometimes a carping attention. We need to give them their due and recognise how such a cluster of talent occurs very seldom in the history of literature in any country.

Given his prolificness, it is inevitable that a *Collected Poems* of Iain Crichton Smith has to be a *Selected Poems*. This *New Collected Poems* is edited with a sympathetic introduction by Matthew McGuire. It follows closely the previous *Collected Poems* (1992) with the addition of a handful of earlier poems, seventy poems from the 1990s and some of Crichton Smith's translations of Sorley MacLean's *Dàin do Eimhir*. To give some indication of the severity of the selection or pruning, the seventy poems from the 1990s represent less than one third of the poetry in the final four volumes. It is in the nature of such enterprises that no editor's choice is likely to match exactly the taste of another reader familiar with the poems. I particularly regret the omission of the Epilogue to *The Leaf and the Marble*, a luminously calm, benedictory conclusion to one of his best volumes, published shortly before his death in 1998.

A question presents itself: why did he write so much? His poetry, like his prose, is often uneven in quality with many unaccommodated jumps in image and register, many awkwardnesses. His mother's Free Church was fond of quoting Jesus's Sermon on the Mount where he says that his true disciples will be known by their fruits. In practical terms, these fruits were often seen as success in the tasks of earning a living; hard work was a matching of God's grace. I was struck by the guilt he seemed to carry for many years that he had not achieved a First Class Degree in Aberdeen. When he came on visits south from Oban, it was as if he had prepared for some examination in what he had been reading and what he had written, as if he was under scrutiny. He identified with notably well-read poets, particularly Auden and Lowell, and admired their daring and versatility in experimenting in different forms and at different levels of intensity. Sometimes there is a desperateness, a verbal frenzy, in his work as if he feared that writing was his only way of giving himself some sense of ordering, of control. Of course, he saw through this notion and one of the prime stimulating tensions in the poetry is between a hope that the poem can be, in Robert Frost's words, 'a momentary stay against confusion' and an awareness of how momentary or even delusive such a stay can be. As he says in his autobiographical book-length poem *A Life*:

> If everything is contingent
> how can the poem
> be made necessary?

And in 'Predestination,' translated from his Gaelic original, he asks a vexing question: 'Calvin tells us we are lost. Freud tells us that we are deceived. O my long thin hands why then are you writing?'

The major recurring theme in the poems is alienation, in many guises. He chooses public figures through whom he explores disjointedness: Kierkegaard, 'Forced theologian of the minimum place' and one of his early exemplars; Hamlet trying to keep his balance in a world of 'warped mirrors'; Orpheus driven mad by isolation and guilt; Van Gogh who cannot 'unlock [himself] from this wheel'; Robinson Crusoe, unclear as to what is actuality and what is fantasy on the island or off it. The intimate presentation of each of their dramas is indicative of Crichton Smith's own precarious hold on sanity at various stages of his life. In the mid-1980s he suffered a severe break-down, fictionally described in his novel *In the Middle of the Wood*. The wood of dislocation, incomprehension and terror is as much the forest of the Grimm brothers as it is Dante's 'selva oscura'. He always had an acute alertness to unexpected congruities and incongruities; the data was unreliable, unstable. For such a mentality, masks and charades can be inordinately threatening. Take, for example, the short poem 'Hallowe'en':

> This small child has an old man's face,
> an old man's clayey bleak unquestioning face.
> He plays the violin and sings a song,
> small, expressionless, unquestioning.
>
> And then after he has played he pulls
> the mask away, and there he stands
> fresh-faced and laughing with blond curls
> and from the grave extends his hands.

On a threshold between the living and the dead, with its mixture of pagan and Christian, and in its Scottish tradition carrying a strong element of the American trick-or-treat, Hallowe'en can be fraught with menace. Crichton Smith questions the unquestioning presentation and the final line delivers a clayey chill. With no religious or political credo to provide him with a secure default position, he has to test all his perceptions on his own thought and feeling and neither can be trusted to offer a comforting assessment of his worth or reliability. For much of his life, 'home' seems to have been a problematic term in an existentialist as well as a personal biographic sense. He tries to explore his thinking on this largest of topics in the long poem (1800 lines), *The Human Face*, published in 1996, two years before his death. In the *New Collected Poems* we have only 150 lines but the whole poem, written in Burns or Habbie Simpson stanzas is, for all its prolixity, well worth reading.

Even in the forty pages of his autobiographical *A Life*, included here in its entirety, one is struck less by his sense of belonging than by a sense of awkwardness and of separation from the situations around him. Neither in his native Lewis nor his National Service nor as a student or as a teacher does he find camaraderie. When he relates how his landlady in Aberdeen 'fills the space around her, holds her stance / against the world's obliquity' he is lamenting what he himself cannot manage:

> I lie in Duthie Park with the *Aeneid*,
> in my white flannels. All the epitaphs shine
> in the adjacent overgrown graveyard.

> LOVE O CARELESS LOVE.

The song heard is the same as in Robert Lowell's 'Skunk Hour', a poem with a similar self-analysis and self-disgust. From the earliest years, Crichton Smith was at odds with his surroundings. He often presented in essays and poems this discordance in relation to his bilingualism in Gaelic and English. What others might have considered a bonus, he often saw as a curse, a homelessness in both languages and the cultures represented by these languages. For his readers (and his stature as a poet), the product is a huge bonus because the poet succeeds in using his personal dilemma to explore with a special insight and sympathy a much wider range of disjuncture and exile. The volume *The Exiles* (1984) contains some excellent poems:

> There is no sorrow worse than this sorrow
> the dumb grief of the exile
> among villages that have strange names
> among the new rocks.
> The shadows are not his home's shadows
> nor the tales his tales

and even the sky is not the same
nor the stars at night.

Having relatives who had emigrated to Canada and Australia helped him
to appreciate the problems of fitting in to a strange place and of coming back
to a place which was no longer what it had been. He uses characters such as
Odysseus and Prospero as examples of displacement and, most tellingly (and
bitterly), he relates the case of the ship *Iolaire* carrying three hundred sailors
home to Lewis at the end of the first world war and which foundered within
sight of the harbour on rocks called the Beasts of Holm. The poem '*Iolaire*'
is narrated by an elder in the Free Church who has to struggle to accommo-
date the tragedy in his religious dispensation.

I do not wish to belittle Crichton Smith's bilingual dilemma or consider
it as only a metaphoric base for his observations on exile. I am sure that the
irony was early appreciated by him of being brought up, a bilingual poet, in
Bayble (alongside his fellow Gaelic poet Derick Thomson). He wrote poems
in Gaelic which no other Gaelic poet of his generation could have written
and found imagery for his poetry in a modern world of gadgets, space travel
and urban living untouched by these contemporaries. Two of his collections
in Gaelic are represented in translation in *New Collected Poems*, including the
intellectually sharp sequence 'The TV':

> Said Plato—
> 'We are tied in a cave'—
> That is the TV.

and

> When he switched off the TV
> the world went out—
> he himself went out.

Despite the extraordinary width of his reading, he did not translate poems
except from Gaelic. His choice of these poems is a very significant facet of
his poetic work. Duncan Ban Macintyre's *Ben Dorain* and the storm section
of Alexander Macdonald's *The Birlinn* are probably the most famous pieces
in Scottish Gaelic but for Crichton Smith they were a challenge and perhaps
an excuse to venture completely beyond his own world and the kinds of
experimental poetry of his time: there is little in the long English tradition

which resembles either of them. For the most part, his translations are much more sinewy and inventive than MacDiarmid's earlier attempts (based on literal translations by Sorley MacLean). In the case of Sorley MacLean's *Dàin do Eimhir* (1943), the younger poet's translations, published in 1971, not only expressed his admiration for the poems and made something of their ambition and power accessible to non-Gaelic readers but allowed Crichton Smith to engage in a passion and a rhetorical richness which did not come naturally to him. Critical opinion is still divided on whether his versions tend to domesticate the stark power of the originals into Movement-style pieces or MacLean's own prose versions convey more of the strangeness, the 'foreignness' of the originals. Although he wrote less in Gaelic in later years his concerns about his first language remained, concerns voiced in his sequence 'Shall Gaelic Die?' (1969):

> He who loses his language loses his world. The
> Highlander who loses his language loses his world.
> The spaceship that goes astray among planets loses the world.
> In an orange world how would you know orange?

In 'For Poets Writing in English over in Ireland', he concludes, quoting a stanza from an early Irish poem:

> And I gaze at the three poets. They are me,
> poised between two languages. They have chosen
> with youth's superb confidence and decision.
>
> 'Half of my side you were, half of my seeing,
> half of my walking you were, half of my hearing.'
> Half of this world I am, half of this dancing.

Is it significant that in English he has a rather fancy name, Iain Crichton Smith, while in Gaelic he is plain Iain Mac A'Ghobhain (Iain Smith)?

Reading through this large swatch of a career, I am struck over and over by the scale of his poetic effort. No subject is too metaphysical or too mundane for his probing explorations. Congruity delighted his mind as much as incongruity, and a comedic awareness gives a particular fizz to many poems. 'In the Chinese Restaurant' and 'Chinese Poem' are typical of his quirky take on how people live their lives. Always there is a striving to find some solid base to place the lever of his mind. Early on, a heroic and stoic Roman pose seemed exemplary against our tawdry and petty concerns. *Deer on the High Hills* (1962) sees the deer as between earth and sky, between a human here and a pure there, in a 'halfway kingdom', but 'Such symbols freeze upon my desolate lips'. In the sixteen sections of *The White Air of March*, the human lot seems helplessly fragmented in bits of quotations and echoes. The Cuillins stand, as they do in Sorley MacLean's poem *The Cuillin*, for a purity, an essence beyond our abilities. In the 1970s the poems become more controlled, more focused, less frenetic, less surreal, but it is only in the final decade of his life that he wins through to a more solidly based contentment. He comes to accept that human love and the imagination together can give not salvation but composure and delight. The imagination had always been there but often of a wilful or clever kind, like Coleridge's Fancy. Later, he recognised (in his poem, 'TV'), 'The narratives overwhelm us, they have no meaning, they have no connection with each other / We need the sacred light of the imagination'. Love came to Crichton Smith later in life. In that wonderful long love poem *The Leaf and the Marble* (1998), he turns against his early bastion, Roman stone: 'When everything trembles, only love holds it together. / Rome is an act of the will, but the leaf protects us'. Rome is even denounced as 'Presbyterian'. In the Epilogue (mentioned earlier), reminiscent of late William Carlos Williams, he reaches a tentative faith:

> So
> love is a finding, in this
> air of summer, a literal
> coming upon, as a bird
> coming into the world
> and finding
>   the faintly provisional.

Jack B. Bedell

Economics

Once, in early fall, I watched my brother
pushpole around the marsh behind our camp
chasing a dogris. He'd hooked the bird by chance,
dumb luck, really, and it had broken his line
just above the cork. Each time we got near it,
the scaup would dive. Then the cork would pop up
thirty yards away. No matter how hard
we poled, we couldn't get there before it was gone.

We'd left the camp at dawn to catch our lunch,
but those speckled trout and striped bass swam
free a foot beneath us in the brackish water
while we poled, well past the time it would've taken
to clean the fish, salt and flour the fillets,
and drop them into a hot, cast-iron skillet.
There would have been time, even, to deglaze the pan
with some mulberry wine and capers for a sauce.

No doubt, my brother and I could've eaten
slowly, had a few beers on the dock, and watched
the sun move across the sky into night
instead of dogging that duck all over creation
for a shad rig. Though what a poor exchange
it would've been for almost catching that cork.

Tony Roberts

Matthew Arnold: A Taste in my Mind

WRITING TO HIS SISTER, FAN, in November 1880, Matthew Arnold was preparing 'A General Introduction' to Thomas Humphry Ward's anthologies, *English Poets*. He had been reading Chaucer, the early French poets and Burns, and wrote, 'But I shall finish with Shakespeare's *King Lear*, before I finally write my Introduction, in order to have a proper taste in my mind while I am at work.' The taste in my mind for Arnold began in spring with a long weekend in the Lakes. The back road from Ambleside to Rydal is a pleasant, undemanding stroll even in rain. I had been reading a little Wordsworth, after dodging the great man for years. Noting that Dr Arnold's holiday home, 'Fox How', lay on the Rydal route, we stopped to photograph it.

I hadn't really read Arnold since school ('Sohrab and Rustum'), aside from 'Dover Beach' and 'The Scholar Gypsy'. In contrast, I have followed an interest in Browning (with moments of Tennyson), which provided enough Victorian poetry for my free time. In that shallow way we have with things that are peripheral to our concerns, I had been put off by Arnold's reputation, an early casualty of the theory wars, and by the fact that he was an educational administrator. I had been a teacher; he a meddler; even his surname seemed out of time.

Yet Arnold is the perfect Victorian to rediscover, since there were so many of him: poet, literary, social and religious critic, educationalist, letter writer, journalist. He was born in 1822, the son of the famous Dr. Arnold of Rugby School. He graduated from Oxford in 1844 and forever held a strong attachment to the university. Although the image of the dandy ('I laugh too much and they make one's laughter mean too much,' as he wrote to one of his friends at 21) Arnold revealed a more serious vein when he first published his poetry in 1849, 1852 and 1853 and became an inspector of schools, a post he held almost to the end of his life, aside from his time as Professor of Poetry at Oxford. His temperament led him into prose criticism, often controversial, which resulted in such works as *Essays in Criticism* (1865 and again in 1888), *Culture and Anarchy* (1869) and *Literature and Dogma* (1873). He died in 1888.

On returning home from Ambleside, I dug out my 1971 copy of the 'Poetry Bookshelf' *Matthew Arnold: Selected Poems and Prose*. I read a handful of poems, followed by Denys Thompson's sympathetic introduction. I admired the fact that Arnold's poetic moods 'tend to be of longing, regret and reflection.' I was cheered by what Thompson referred to as Arnold's negative influence: 'having left matters of classroom technique to teachers'. I began to rethink.

I was taken by the heartbreaking children's verse, 'The Forsaken Merman', as I was to be later by the Odyssean return, 'The Strayed Reveller'. The former's reworking of a Danish tale prefigures the Arnolds' loss of three of their boys, if one transposes the grief at a mother's returning to land:

> Come away, away children.
> Come children, come down!
> The hoarse wind blows colder;
> Lights shine in the town.

In contrast to the stoicism here, there is something self-pitying in Arnold's portrayal of the poet's lot in 'The Strayed Reveller':

> These things, Ulysses,
> The wise bards also
> Behold and sing.
> But oh, what labour!
> Oh prince, what pain!

On a whim, I had recently bought a copy of the Penguin *Matthew Arnold: Selected Prose*. It led me to the 'Preface to the First Edition of Poems 1853', 'On the Modern Element in Literature 1857' (an essay I had referred to when reviewing Adam Kirsch's superb book, *The Modern Element*, for *Agenda*), 'The Function of Criticism at the Present Time' and 'The Study of Poetry'. It was an entrée to what George Saintsbury described—in a flourish of 1891—as Arnold's 'literary grace and girlish charm'.

'The Function of Criticism at the Present Time' appealed to the critic I aspired to be. It demanded that 'criticism must be sincere, simple, flexible, ardent, ever widening its knowledge.' It also made this, still often ignored, point: 'By the very nature of things, as England is not all the world, much of the best that is known and thought in the world cannot be of English growth, must be foreign ... The English critic of literature, therefore, must dwell much on foreign thought ...'

Arnold is often more rhetorical than analytical and, whilst one might applaud his definition of criticism as 'a disinterested endeavour to learn and propagate the best that is known and thought in the world', it has raised more questions than it answers. It also painted a rather large bullseye on his reputation.

Such an 'endeavour' requires, he suggests, 'establishing an author's place in literature, and his relation to a central standard (and if this is not done, how are we to get at our *best in the world?*)'. This canonical urge has been much reviled in our time as a form of paternalism and oppression. Nevertheless it is a prime example of Arnold's moral seriousness.

'The Study of Poetry' opened the posthumously published *Essays in Criticism: Second Series* (1888). There are acute insights in the essays on such poets as Wordsworth ('His poetry is the reality, his philosophy ... the illusion') and Byron ('True, he has no light, cannot lead us from the past to the future; "the moment he reflects, he is a child,"' Arnold writes, citing Goethe). There are also gorgeously inappropriate moments, such as this on Shelley: 'beautiful and ineffectual angel, beating in the void his luminous wings in vain.'

In 'The Study of Poetry', however, the author also makes at least one stirring, aspirational pronouncement: 'More and more mankind will discover that we have to turn to poetry to interpret life for us, to console us, to sustain us. Without poetry, our science will appear incomplete; and most of what now passes with us for religion and philosophy will be replaced by poetry.' Arnold's statement of belief is followed by a caveat with dramatic consequences for his own poetry: 'But if we conceive thus highly of the destinies of poetry, we must also set our standard for poetry high, since poetry, to be capable of fulfilling such high destinies, must be poetry of a high order of excellence.'

So, in the 'Preface to the First Edition of Poems 1853', he explains the omission of his poem 'Empedocles at Etna': it is 'poetically faulty' in creating a situation 'in which the suffering finds no vent in action'. Later he defended himself against a perceived classical bias in the 'Preface to the Second Edition of Poems' (1854): 'It has been said that I wish to limit the poet, in his choice of subjects, to the period of Greek and Roman antiquity; but it is not so. I only counsel him to choose for his subjects great actions, without regarding to what time they belong.'

The penalty of high, misguided ambition can be harsh. Did it lead to Arnold's poetic silence? In a curious attempt for immediacy, Lionel Trilling writes in the present tense, in his *Matthew Arnold* (1939): 'He is only forty-five when his last volume appears.' That led me to Ian Hamilton's *A Gift Imprisoned: the Poetic Life of Matthew Arnold* (1998), which preoccupies itself with Arnold's switch in mid-career to prose when the poetic seam played out. As Hamilton plausibly if not entirely convincingly explains, Arnold's epic ambition for poetry—'great creative epochs in literature are so rare,' he had once written—obviated his own lyric talent, which he considered to be altogether too personal and hardly, therefore, in the public interest. Arnold wrote what might be viewed as a testament with the words: 'More and more I feel bent against the modern English habit (too much encouraged by Wordsworth) of using poetry as a channel for thinking aloud, instead of making anything.'

Yet in a sense Hamilton's reading of the end of talent flatters Matthew Arnold. While the latter's views were honestly held and reflected his great ambition for poetry, they also rationalised his disappointment. There are two relevant considerations here, touched upon by the late Mick Imlah in a 1998 *TLS* review of Hamilton's book. Firstly, as to Hamilton's thesis of the burnt-out poet: the murky nature of Arnold's publishing makes it difficult to date all poems; secondly—more persuasively—with the life he chose to lead it was hard for him to concentrate on poetry. I believe Arnold simply made what were, for him, the more attractive choices. He needed to make a living; he felt his mission to lie in castigating his peers in prose ('the elegant Jeremiah' he was dubbed); he wanted this public life as well as a social life; he had already established his poetic credentials—despite whatever reservations. Besides, he could always write poetry in private moments.

Was he a contented man? My next step was to buy a cradle-to-grave biography, Nicholas Murray's excellent, *A Life of Matthew Arnold* (1996), an account that admires its author. Matthew Arnold 'was indeed the most delightful of companions,' G. W. E. Russell had written in *Portraits of the Seventies*; 'a man of the world entirely free from worldliness and a man of letters without the faintest trace of pedantry.' Murray presents the reader with exactly such a figure, whilst also maintaining his focus on the seriousness of Arnold's concern: 'His cultural optimism was rooted in one thing—reiterated so many times in so many contexts that we should call it his basic philosophy of life—and that was that moral virtue and the desire for the best in art alike derived their motivating power from "the instinct of self-preservation in humanity"'.

Pursuing such mental equilibrium, I turned again to Lionel Trilling's *Matthew Arnold*, a study of the poet's thought in its time. Trilling cites Arnold's wish that the critic had to be the *'undulating and diverse* being of Montaigne' as Trilling himself generally has been. Here, however, though the early part of the book is compelling 'as a biography of Arnold's mind' it cannot avoid 'the pitfalls of interpretive biography'. Trilling may not, for instance, attempt to solve the paradox of the serious dandy in young Arnold yet he cannot help but toss his 'interpretive' hat into the ring again and again. At this juncture, Park Honan's biography arrived: *Matthew Arnold: A*

Life. I was excited at the prospect of reading Honan's book, since I treasure the excellent biography of Browning he completed after William Irvine's death. Here though the focus is at times choked with detail ('I have tried to find every known fact relating to Arnold'), particularly up to Arnold's marriage—not uninteresting, but taking us off the narrative path. A good example is his exploration and anti-climactic 'revelation' of the identity of the 'Marguerite' of the Switzerland poems. The reader admires Honan's pursuit of 'an authentic sense of Arnold's own historical present', but becomes increasingly aware that this involves some degree of imaginative intrusion.

Honan's boldest claim is one of his first: 'An understanding of him is really more useful to us than an understanding of any other Englishman of the last century.' I found a partial explanation of this stance amongst the gems in the essays edited by Kenneth Allott on Matthew Arnold (*Writers and their Backgrounds*, 1975), firstly in the opening essay by an American professor of mine, Fraser Neiman: 'Arnold's centrality to our understanding of his age resides partly in the range of his interests, partly in the seriousness with which he sought answers to his questionings, and partly also in his feeling for the unitary character of European culture.'

What he turned to was the 'stabilising centre in his conviction of the absoluteness of ethical values'. Edmond Scherer, the nineteenth century French critic, would have agreed. In an essay on 'Wordsworth and Modern Poetry', he wrote:

> Mr. Arnold, who is far from endowing himself with any kind of mission, who is the simplest and least affected of men, has none the less become in his own country the representative of the higher function of letters. No one has recognised their humanising influence as he has, and no one was so fit as he to become the apostle of what I may call intellectual civilisation. At the present moment Mr. Arnold is the most seductive product that English literature has to offer, by reason of his union of thought and fancy, of solidity and grace, of self-respect and liberty of mind.

One certainly comes under the sway of Arnold, of what Henry James called his 'European accent'—agree with him or not—and it is probably because, as John Holloway identified in his 1953 book, *The Victorian Sage: Studies in Argument*: 'If he offers anything of wisdom or sanity or mental poise, it is to be found in the whole experience of reading him, in a sense of what intellectual urbanity is that transpires rather from his handling of problems than from his answers to them. He mediates not a view of the world, but a habit of mind…'

To his mother, Arnold once explained that he was 'determined in print to be always scrupulously polite. The bane of English reviewing and newspaper writing is, and has always been, its *grossièreté.*' Yet as he admitted to his sister, Fan, in one letter: 'I always feel that the public is not disposed to take me cordially; it receives my things … with more astonishment than pleasure at first.' Unsurprising, when one considers how frequently he attacked his own middle class as 'Philistines'. Never a man to avoid repetition of phrases and ideas, he seems to have relished damning: 'our world of an aristocracy materialized and null, a middle-class purblind and hideous, a lower class crude and brutal'.

A moral crusader, then? In an essay in the Allott collection R.H. Super makes the extreme claim that the Arnold we have is most original because he was 'not exclusively, not even primarily, a literary man.' His interest lay in education, politics, society, religion. With that in mind, I needed to give some thought to Arnold as social thinker, since all his poetry criticism leads in that direction. I bought *Culture and Anarchy* (1869) in the edition edited by Stefan Collini, stirred by the above and by Arnold's comment in *Mixed Essays*: 'Whoever seriously occupies himself with literature will soon perceive its vital connexion with other agencies.' In his introduction to *Culture and Anarchy*, Collini sums up the self-satisfied Liberal ethos of the time which 'had no room for "high ideals" or notions of a "best self", still less for seeing these embodied in a conception of "the state" as the highest expression of the national community. *Culture and Anarchy* was a bravura attempt to domesticate these alien notions and to make such elevated language part of the common currency of English thought.'

What is most inspiring in the book is Arnold's notion that his conception of culture, in its pursuit of perfection ('of sweetness and light'), does not seek to talk down to 'the masses', but 'seeks to do away with classes; to make the best that has been thought and known in the world current everywhere.' This is the most slyly forgotten of all Matthew Arnold ideas. If he was habitually patrician, he was also a democrat.

I now began to search out Arnold's more private voice. Via cheap old copies, I plunged into the letters, the two volumes collected by George W. E. Russell in 1895, *Letters of Matthew Arnold, 1849–88*; Arnold Whitridge's slim *Unpublished Letters of Matthew Arnold* (1923) and *The Letters of Matthew Arnold to Arthur Hugh Clough*, edited by Howard Foster Lowry in 1932. They include Arnold's famous self-assessment as a poet, written to his mother in 1869: 'My poems represent, on the whole, the main movement of mind of the last quarter of a century, and thus they will probably have their day as people become conscious to themselves of what that movement of mind is, and interested in the literary productions which reflect it. It might be fairly urged that I have less poetical sentiment than Tennyson, and less intellectual vigour and abundance than Browning; yet, because I have perhaps more of a fusion of the two than either of them, and have more regularly applied that fusion to the main line of modern development, I am likely enough to have my turn, as they have had theirs.'

Aside from revealing confidence in his modern Victorian mind, this suggests that Arnold clearly felt that he had done enough to secure a high poetic reputation. It is sobering, then, that Arnold Whitridge was lamenting in 1923—only thirty five years after Arnold's death—that, 'to the average college student of to-day he belongs as irretrievably to the past as Pope or Dryden.'

When George W. E. Russell wrote in his 'Prefatory Note' of the naturalness of these letters ('They are, in a word, *himself*') he explained that Arnold's family had wished them in print to reveal 'his tenderness and playfulness and filial affection'. The letters to Clough put back a little starch. Arthur Hugh Clough had been Dr. Arnold's favourite pupil, almost four years older than the poet. Although disappointing his friends' expectations of his literary accomplishments, he had nevertheless produced the wonderful *Amours de Voyage*. The letters are a selection from the correspondence between the two, beginning in 1845 when Arnold was 23 and only ending in 1861 with Clough's death in Florence. If Arnold undervalued Clough's poetry, he loved the immense talent and the man. Inevitably, his letters reveal a great deal about himself. In September 1849, for instance: 'What I must tell you is that I have never yet succeeded in any one great occasion in consciously mastering myself ... (my) one natural craving is not for profound thoughts, mighty spiritual workings etc. etc. but a distinct seeing of my way as far as my own nature is concerned.'

There is also the pessimism, which goes deeper than any touch of affectation: 'My dearest Clough these are damned times—everything is against one—the height to which knowledge is come, the spread of luxury, our physical enervation, the absence of great *natures*, the unavoidable contact with millions of small ones, newspapers, cities, light profligate friends, moral desperadoes like Carlyle, our own selves, and the sickening consciousness of our difficulties.'

At Clough's death Arnold wrote to his widow, 'the impression he left was one of those which deepen with time and such as I never expect again to experience.' Clough's death led me to Arnold's 'Thyrsis', a curiously impersonal monody modelled on 'The Scholar Gypsy' and recounting, in the pastoral tradition, their bachelor love of wandering the 'Cumner Hill Side', west of Oxford:

> But Thyrsis never more we swains shall see;
>   See him come back, and cut a smoother reed,
>   And blow a strain the world at last shall heed—
> For Time, not Corydon, hath conquered thee!

My least immediately useful purchase became *The Note-Books of Matthew Arnold*. I have only picked at this enigmatic collection, 37 years in the making. The entries are in English, and (untranslated) French, German, Italian, Latin and Greek. They include lists of quotations from writers that inspired Arnold or prompted thoughts, many repeated, many religious, as well as reading lists and engagements. Though according to his daughter, Arnold believed that someone who collected the quotations might produce a 'volume of priceless worth', as the Preface dryly observes, 'Not all are from the best that has been known and thought in the world'. Perhaps most interesting are the reading and writing intentions. In 1880, for example, Arnold hoped to write a 'Preface to Ward's Poets', as well as on Gray, Keats, on copyright, 'The Future of Liberalism' and Byron, whereas his intended reading list is getting on for a hundred works. In an 1882 letter he wrote: 'The importance of reading, not slight stuff to get through the time, but the best that has been written, forces itself upon me more and more every year I live; it is living in good company, the best company, and people are generally quite keen enough, or too keen, about doing that, yet they do not do it in the simplest and best manner by reading.'

When Lionel Trilling observed, of the Arnold of the note-books, 'he had what must seem to us an almost primitive belief in "wisdom"', one wonders if that is such a bad thing.

For atmosphere, I next bought a first edition of *New Poems* (1867), a bright green book with brown end papers and gilt lettering. It cost me £40 or so and when I sat with it I was first delighted to see that 'Dover Beach' ('the greatest single poem of the Victorian period', according to Michael Schmidt) was bookended by two slight but charming lyrics, 'Calais Sands' and 'The Terrace at Berne'. Here is Arnold's winning clarity of feeling and expression: the lover's dreaming detail of his loved one's presence in the former poem; the 'crucible of time' in the latter which may obliterate traces of the loved one, or else allow a reunion:

> Ah, shall I see thee, while a flush
> Of startled pleasure floods thy brow,
> Quick through the oleanders brush,
> And clap thy hands, and cry: 'Tis thou!

I also found poems I had previously overlooked, such as 'Balder Dead', in Kenneth Allott's *The Poems of Matthew Arnold* (part of Longmans Annotated English Poets series—a wonderful resource). 'Balder Dead' is a tale of skulduggery from Teutonic myth, which Arnold felt Virgilian in its diction and rhythm. The end of the poem, for example, where the disconsolate Hermod must leave his friends to death, has a wonderful final antithesis:

> And as a stork which idle boys have trapped,
> And tied him in a yard, at autumn sees
> Flocks of his kind pass flying o'er his head
> To warmer lands, and coasts that keep the sun;
> He strains to join their flight, and from his shed
> Follows them with a long complaining cry—
> So Hermod gazed, and yearned to join his kin.

> At last he sighed, and set forth back to Heaven.

To avoid hagiography, let me suggest another perspective on the man and his legacy. Firstly, there is the description by Logan Pearsall Smith I found in an essay by the great Edmund Wilson. The earlier American essayist had met a number of celebrated people and Wilson gives us one subversive reminiscence:

> it makes tangible the Philistine one had suspected in a great preacher against the Philistines to find out that Matthew Arnold presented himself to the boarders in a Dresden pension, who did not yet know who he was, as 'a tall figure in a suit of large checks, with a broad face and black whiskers,' marching in 'with the jaunty air of an English schoolmaster who, in travelling abroad, assumes what he considers a man-of-the world

deportment'; that he used to regale his fellow boarders 'with an account of the very favourable reception he had received at the Saxon court from certain dear princesses who were his especial friends; and that he remarked in an off-hand way that *The Valkyrie* had struck him as 'the sort of thing I should have composed myself if I happened to try my hand at composing music.'

Secondly, we see the perils of probity where I have come to a temporary stop, in Stefan Collini's excellent, slim, *Matthew Arnold: A Critical Portrait.* A man like Arnold, who courted controversy, invited misrepresentation. Whilst his name echoes through cultural debate, the misrepresentations are habitual, paradoxically amongst his keenest supporters.

The right-Arnoldians, according to Collini, are those reactionary, canonical types who dress their antagonism to modernity in his authority. They love Arnold for his commitment to hermetically sealed standards and texts. The left-Arnoldians are those who quietly shelve the master's actual pronouncements, whilst applauding the fact of his critiquing his contemporaries. I would suggest that one might adopt a non-polarising model. For instance, one might approve of his commitment to a canon, provided it is periodically re-energised by fine works from the sexes and the minorities.

There are all the others, certainly, who take Walt Whitman's negative estimate that Arnold will not be missed, that he was 'one of the dudes of Literature.' There are those who are irritated by his pronouncements or merely ignore them. Yet Matthew Arnold's poetry and his contribution to establishing the art of constructive criticism are of real importance, whatever the inconsistencies of his positions and the limitation of his vision. The wellspring of the former he expressed in his essay on 'Maurice de Guérin':

> The grand power of poetry is its interpretative power; by which I mean, not a power of drawing out in black and white an explanation of the mystery of the universe, but the power of so dealing with things as to awaken in us a wonderfully full, new, and intimate sense of them, and of our relations with them.

Such thoughts have given me a taste in my mind for Arnold these past few months.

Julie Kane

Mortality and Mellowing: On Wendy Cope

ALMOST TWENTY YEARS AGO an American reviewing a book by Cope for a transatlantic readership remarked that Cope was not very well known in the U.S. but almost 'too well-known' in Britain. Not much has changed since then. Although Cope is one of the best-selling poets in the British Isles and the winner of a BBC Radio poll to determine their listeners' choice for Poet Laureate, Cope's books can be difficult to obtain in the United States, even through online booksellers. Faced with a wait of five to six weeks delivery time from Amazon, this reviewer had to ask *The Dark Horse* to buy and mail her a copy so that the transit time did not chew up all of her review-writing time, while an American friend writing an academic essay about Cope had to ask a relative to bring a copy home from London packed in her suitcase.

In the Age of the Internet, difficulties in getting one's hands on the physical artifact of a book should, in theory, pose no barrier to the dissemination of individual poems across international boundaries. But because Cope can actually get paid fairly well for her poems, she has campaigned against their unauthorized posting on the Internet and against the practice of reading poets' works aloud in public without first clearing copyright permissions. As she has noted, 'short funny poems' like hers are particularly vulnerable to such well-meaning pirates. While those of us whose annual poetry royalties could probably be paid out in rolls of postage stamps normally rejoice when an amateur blogger puts one of our poems online, Cope phones her attorneys—well, she does so for the worst offenders, which tends to scare off the small fry. One such website, which had contained about twenty of Cope's poems, now bears only the foreboding message 'Poems removed upon request from the legal representatives of the Poet.' Ironically, for a poet somewhat at war with the Internet, Cope has just sold her archive of emails dating back to 2004 to the British Library for the sum of £32,000 ($53,000).

Logistically difficult as it may be for the American half of this audience to catch up to the British half, I would recommend that potential readers of Cope's new book begin by acquainting themselves with her first book, *Making Cocoa for Kingsley Amis*. Not to do so would be like reading the later poems of Robert Frost without knowing his early work. The Frost of *In the Clearing* (1962), genial and wise and upbeat ('Forgive, O Lord, my little

Family Values by Wendy Cope. Faber and Faber Ltd, 2011. ISBN 978-0-571-27421-5, £12.99, 66 pp, hbk.

jokes on Thee / And I'll forgive Thy great big one on me'), is all the more
to be treasured if one knows the darkness of *A Boy's Will, North of Boston,*
and *Mountain Interval.* In both early Frost and early Cope, one is struck by a
wildness, a bleakness, a runaway self-destructive tendency that is just barely
kept in check by the exquisite formal control of the art. It is like listen-
ing to music played on bagpipes or Cajun accordion, with that mournful
drone note always fused to the melody, however tuneful. Of course, one
can't keep up that level of intensity throughout a lifetime. Other such artists
flamed out early, but these two mellowed out.

Wendy Cope, for her part, burst on the British poetry scene in 1986
with a first book that violated nearly every prevailing trend in contemporary poetry. Transgression #1: Poets were not supposed to write in rhyme
and meter. Cope did so, expertly. Transgression #2: Poetry was not supposed to be funny. Cope was pee-in-your-pants funny much of the time.
Transgression #3: Women poets were supposed to stand in awe of the Great
White Male tradition of English poetry. Cope's book contained poems paro-
dying or mocking GWMs including Shakespeare, Wordsworth, Eliot, Larkin,
Hughes, Heaney, and Raine. Worst of all, perhaps, was Transgression #4:
Poetry is not supposed to be popular. But while the average print run for a
book of contemporary poetry is about five hundred to a thousand copies,
Cope's books sold briskly from the outset, and to date their sales have topped
the half-million mark.

In the case of Frost, a vast swath of the reading public responded to
his modernism before most critics did, and the same is true of Cope and
her postmodernism. Academics who dismissed her work as 'traditional'
while believing that poets writing anecdotal free-verse lyrics in the style
of William Carlos Williams were somehow hip or trendy were missing
the obvious. Cope had no consistent formal 'voice.' Like many postmodern architects and musical composers, Cope was borrowing and recycling
forms from the past with no particular allegiance to them: the villanelle,
the triolet, the ballade. She used them like handkerchiefs for the purpose
at hand—not terribly concerned about re-laundering them for future use,
although that could happen. Part of the fun was the contrast between the
'tradition' associated with each form and Cope's irreverent content. She
also mixed brand names of pop culture consumer products with allusions
to Shakespeare and Tacitus. Like many funny women from Dorothy Parker
forward, she adopted the persona of a woman on the margins of polite society. The 'I' of those poems drank too much, jumped into bed with awful
men and got dumped by them, craved cigarettes, and thumbed her nose at

the rich and the royals. But she also wrote poems from the perspective of 'Jason Strugnell,' a failed and pretentious male poet. Her use of the Strugnell alter ego, as well as the ease with which she parodied the voices and styles of many famous male poets, could serve as textbook illustrations of the decentered postmodern self, not to mention the destabilization of gender binaries. One critic, Marta Perez Novales, has examined Cope's work in relation to Frederic Jameson's definitions of parody versus pastiche, but other than Novales, many academics seem to have mistaken Cope's stylistic timeliness for its opposite, anachronism.

Having paid homage to Cope's early brilliance, one can proceed to consider *Family Values* in its proper context, as a later stage in her development. The very title of the volume poses somewhat of a puzzle: is it ironic, or not? The phrase 'family values' has remained in the news since at least the early 1990s, signifying a Republican or conservative party platform that views the Christian, heterosexual marriage with children (and without adultery, abortion, or divorce) as the foundation of civic culture. Had Cope used that title on one of her earlier books, the sly wink would have been obvious. In this book the phrase appears in the poem 'The Archers and Adultery,' about a BBC radio soap opera, and there, too, Cope intends it to be hypocritical: 'Yes, in *The Archers* family values reign. / The straying spouses all come back again.' Yet *Family Values* does seem to embrace family values to a certain extent. The book opens with four poems about churchgoing or Christianity, and Cope told Tom Payne in a recent interview in *The Daily Telegraph* that she had returned to the Church of England after a long period of absence. Many of the poems celebrate the quiet domesticity of a contented love relationship, mirroring the happiness that Cope has found in her own personal life with poet-critic and biographer Lachlan Mackinnon.

Lest anyone think that Cope has gone over to the dark side—or, perhaps more accurately, the light side—she also told Payne that she had been lured back to church by evensong services, and that 'I was so moved by it I tried to persuade myself that I believed it all. I almost succeeded.' In 'An Anniversary Poem,' Cope tweaks the Church of England for refusing to allow women to become bishops. And when she does zero in on particular families in *Family Values*, they are (thank goodness) miserably dysfunctional. Several poems are written from the perspective of a child with an extremely overbearing mother, and Cope told Payne that her own mother's death in 2004 had enabled her to publish some of these poems for the first time. The mother in these lines is always convinced that she is right, even when she is dead wrong; she worries so much about what others will think that she tells her daughter to stay home from church rather than attend without taking communion. The speaker's mother is ashamed of her bus driver brother's occupation, and she packs her daughter off to a boarding school where she is bullied by the other girls. If these summaries are not sounding at all like the 'typical' Cope poem with wit and rhymes snapping like mousetraps all the way through, that's because they are not. The majority of the poems in the volume are free verse, and the prevailing tone is serious.

The average American poetry book, these days, seems to get planned more carefully than the average American military engagement. It has become increasingly fashionable for the whole thing to tell a story or center around a theme. There must be a dramatic 'arc' from beginning to end, and within each individual section there must be a smaller arc—arcs within arcs. Then, based upon research from neuroscience showing that the last thing in a series makes the strongest impression, and the first thing in a series makes the second-strongest impression, one's strongest poems must be positioned in the key slots within the mini-arcs. By comparison, baseball team managers have it easy, dealing with only nine players and easy issues like where to position one's strongest hitter and fastest base-stealer within a starting lineup. If you can't structure the manuscript yourself, there are even consultants who will do it for you, for a fee.

But the U.K. approach to assembling a manuscript still seems to be, 'Hey, here are some poems I wrote since my last book'—rather a relief in contrast to American overdeterminism. *Family Values* appears to consist of a bunch of poems Cope wrote because she felt like it, followed by a bunch of poems she wrote because she was commissioned to do so. Still, within the first section, one can follow a progression of themes: Christianity and the Church, an overbearing mother and a miserable childhood, time and loss, the looming fact of mortality, the transience of happiness. The act of writing as an attempt to capture what will otherwise be lost is a recurring motif. While Cope has parodied Shakespeare's Sonnet 55 in the past (in Cope's version, 'Not only marble, but the plastic toys / From cornflake packets will outlive this rhyme'), in this book she seems to be rewriting it again and again. Finding herself in tears before a portrait of a long-dead bride and groom, Cope's speaker thinks, 'Someone will read our story, by and by. / Perhaps they'll feel like this. Perhaps they'll cry' ('Dutch Portraits'). Re-encountering an old flame at a poetry conference, another speaker imagines the future in which one of them will hear of the death of the other: 'The survivor will sit down and weep / And write a poem mourning the ex-lover / And have a drink or two and go to sleep.'

Note the self-reflexive gestures within those two quotations, the poet calling attention to the fact that she is writing the poem—another post-modern technique of Cope's (although the sixteenth-century Bard certainly employed it, too). 'Look at how I write,' she observes in 'Boarders.' 'And now / I've gone and put her in a poem,' she says of a childhood friend ('Omo'). Sitting 'In the Wimpy Bar at Stafford services,' Cope's speaker imagines that she could be taken for several identities including 'A poet, maybe, scribbling in her notebook.' In 'At the Poetry Conference,' she says, 'I need to write a poem but I've written it / Already' and, 'You see I'm alternating / Two kinds of rhyme, the way you recommend.' Disarmed of her usual humor and formal armor, Cope may be leaning more heavily than usual on this technique for its effect of distancing the writer from the painful material of the poem. John Gardner in *The Art of Fiction* famously advised that a writer should never awaken a reader from the dream cast by the narrative, but here Cope is dashing ice water on her reader every few minutes and calling out, 'It's not a bad dream—just a poem!'

Surprisingly, because this reviewer did not think Cope's commissioned *The River Girl* (1991) or 'The Teacher's Tale' (2000) the equal of her 'self-commissioned' work, some of the most delightful poems in this collection are to be found in the second section. There are nine poems from 'The Audience,' a series commissioned by the Endellion String Quartet, and eight from 'An ABC of the BBC,' a sequence written under the patronage of BBC Radio 4. 'The Audience' consists of dramatic monologues spoken by various audience members and musicians involved in an orchestral concert, from the players stuck in traffic to 'The Cougher' and the couple on their first date, each presuming the other to be a classical music expert and hoping not to be exposed as a pretender. The poems read well on the page, but they would work even better staged by actors, with musical accompaniment. Some of the wittiest poems in the volume can be found in 'from An ABC of the BBC,' perhaps because the domestically contented poet, unable to unearth much fodder for satire in her own life, finds plenty of it in pop culture radio programming and its middle-class audiences. For example, among the '[t]hings that make me switch the radio off' are 'Actors being actorish, and, worse, / The voice of Dylan Thomas reading verse.'

With Cope herself always ready to plunge a sharp pen into the balloon of anyone's pretentiousness, it seems rather foolhardy to pose the question: How many of the poems in *Family Values* will stand with Cope's best and most memorable poems of the past, on a par with 'Waste Land Limericks,'

'Triolet' ('I used to think all poets were Byronic'), 'From June to December,' 'Rondeau Redoublé' ('There are so many kinds of awful men'), the Strugnell poems, 'Bloody Men,' 'Loss,' 'Another Unfortunate Choice,' 'Valentine,' 'Flowers,' 'I Worry,' 'Two Cures for Love,' 'Favourite,' 'Being Boring,' 'What I Think,' 'The Sorrow of Socks'?—and that's just a top-of-the-head list, by no means complete. Perhaps the pretty little triolet 'Stars,' reminiscent of Whitman's 'When I First Heard the Learn'd Astronomer'; in both poems, there is more to be gained from gazing in delight at the night sky than from studying facts about it or looking to it for deeper meaning. And perhaps, the two-poem sequence 'Differences of Opinion,' although it is not really new: the first poem was previously published in *If I Don't Know* (2001), and both poems appeared in Cope's 2008 volume of new and selected works, *Two Cures for Love*. This is not an album studded with potential Greatest Hits, but everything this poet does is worth following with close attention. Wendy Cope is a living treasure. So say I, and so say the folk.

Dick Davis

Wil Mills

Once in a speeding car at night, I heard
Your voice sing out, plangent and weirdly strong
In a wailing country *a capella*,
Yeats's 'He Wishes for the Cloths of Heaven.'

So vigorous and vulnerable the sound,
As if an adolescent angry angel
Were suddenly beside us in the dark,
Defiant and admonishing, afraid.

Editor's note: the gifted American poet and singer-songwriter Wilmer Mills died in his early forties on 25 July, 2011. An appreciation will follow in a future issue of *The Dark Horse*.

NOTES ON CONTRIBUTORS

CLAIRE ASKEW's work won the William Sharpe Hunter Memorial Scholarship in 2008 for her MSc in Creative Writing at the University of Edinburgh. She is the author of a pamphlet collection, *The Mermaid and the Sailors* (Red Squirrel, 2011), and teaches at Edinburgh's Telford College and the University of Edinburgh.

JACK B. BEDELL teaches at Southeastern Louisiana University where he also serves as editor of *Louisiana Literature* and director of Louisiana Literature Press. His most recent books are *Call and Response* and *Come Rain, Come Shine*, both from Texas Review Press.

NIALL CAMPBELL is from the island of South Uist and in 2011 received an Eric Gregory Award from the Society of Authors, and a Robert Louis Stevenson Fellowship from Creative Scotland. His first pamphlet will be released by Happen*Stance* Press in early 2012.

DICK DAVIS's latest book of his own poetry is *A Trick of Sunlight* (Anvil, 2007). He is a Professor of Persian at Ohio State University and probably the pre-eminent translator of poetry from that tongue.

DANA GIOIA, formerly the Head of the National Endowment for the Arts, is the Judge Widney Professor of Poetry and Public Culture at the University of South California. His fourth book of poems will be published by Graywolf Press in Spring 2012.

SEÁN HALDANE works as a consultant clinical neuropsychologist in London. His *Always Two: Collected Poems 1966–2009* (Greenwich Exchange, 2009) was reviewed in issue 25 of *The Dark Horse*.

KEVIN HANSON lives in Sheffield and has had poems published in several magazines.

A. B. JACKSON works for the NHS in Glasgow. His *Apocrypha* was the Poetry Book Society's pamphlet Choice for Summer 2011.

JULIE KANE is Poet Laureate of Louisiana for 2011–2013. Her two most recent poetry collections are *Jazz Funeral* (2009), David Mason's choice for the Donald Justice Poetry Prize, and *Rhythm & Booze* (2003), Maxine Kumin's selection for the National Poetry Series and a Poets' Prize finalist.

ANGELA LEIGHTON is Senior Research Fellow at Trinity College, Cambridge. Her first book of poems, *A Cold Spell*, was published in 2000, and her second, *Sea Level*, appeared in 2007.

KONA MACPHEE recently won the Geoffrey Faber Memorial Prize for her second collection of poems, *Perfect Blue* (Bloodaxe, 2010). Born in Australia, she now lives in Perthshire.

ALASDAIR MACRAE is a former Senior Lecturer in English Studies at the University of Stirling. Among other things, he was close friends with many poets of the Scottish Renaissance. His latest book is a critical monograph on Norman MacCaig (Northcote House Publishers, 2010).

RICHIE MCCAFFERY has a pamphlet of work due out from Happen*Stance* Press in March 2012 and will also appear in Todd Swift's 'Young British Poets' anthology for Oxfam in early 2012. He is a Carnegie Scholar at the University of Glasgow, researching the Scottish Poetry of World War Two.

MARCIA MENTER is a contributing editor to *The Dark Horse*. Her pamphlet *The Longing Machine* was published by Happen*Stance* Press in 2007.

TRAVIS MOSSOTTI's first collection of poems, *About the Dead* (Utah State University Press, 2011), was awarded the 2011 May Swenson Poetry Award by contest judge Garrison Keillor.

KATRINA NAOMI is a poet based in south London and is originally from Margate. Her first full collection was *The Girl with the Cactus Handshake* (Templar Poetry, 2009). During 2009–2010, Katrina was the first Writer in Residence at the Bronte Parsonage Museum in Haworth, Yorkshire.

HELENA NELSON runs Happen*Stance* Press in Scotland. Her latest collection of poems, *Plot and Counter-plot*, was published by Shoestring Press in 2010.

DENNIS O'DRISCOLL's eight books of poetry include *New and Selected Poems* (Anvil Press, 2004) and *Reality Check* (Anvil, 2007). Among other publications are *Troubled Thoughts, Majestic Dreams: Selected Prose Writings* (Gallery Press, 2001) and *Stepping Stones: Interviews with Seamus Heaney* (Faber, 2008).

TONY ROBERTS's third book of poems, *Outsiders*, was published in 2010 by Shoestring Press.

PHILIP RUSH has a delightful small studio overlooking fields, but poems don't like it. They tend to arrive when he is walking, driving a car, or drinking coffee in a gorgeous small café near Paddington Station.

KAY RYAN's *Odd Blocks: Selected and New Poems*, will be reviewed in issue 28. She was the U.S. Poet Laureate from 2008 to 2010, and won a Pulitzer Prize for Poetry in April, 2011.

ROBERT SELBY's poems have appeared in the *Times Literary Supplement*, the *Guardian online*, and elsewhere. A selection featured in the recent anthology, *Days of Roses*. He lives in Kent.

ANNE STEVENSON is a past winner of the The Poetry Foundation's Neglected Masters Award, the Lannan Lifetime Achievement Award for Poetry and the Northern Rock Foundation Writer's Award. Her *Selected Poems* was published in the Library of America series in 2008.

RORY WATERMAN's poems will be included in selection this year in *New Poetries V* (Carcanet). He co-edits *New Walk Magazine* and writes regularly for a number of literary publications. He is completing a PhD at the University of Leicester, and lives in Bristol.

RICHARD WILBUR turned 90 earlier this year. His latest book of poems, *Anterooms*, was published by Houghton Mifflin Harcourt in 2010.